The Purposed Woman

Transformational Truths for Purposeful Living

HOPE D. BLACKWELL

Copyright © 2012 by Hope D. Blackwell.

All rights reserved. No part of this book may be used or reproduced by any means, graphic, electronic, or mechanical, including photocopying, recording, taping or by any information storage retrieval system without the written permission of the publisher except in the case of brief quotations embodied in critical articles and reviews.

Scripture quotations are taken from the Hebrew Greek Key Word Study Bible—KJV, copyright © 1984, 1991, used by permission of AMG International Inc., Chattanooga, TN; and the Dake Annotated Reference Bible, copyright 1963, 1991, used by permission of Dake Publishing, Lawrenceville, GA.

Scripture quotations identified as (KJV) are taken from the King James Version of the Bible. Those identified as (NKJV) are taken from the New King James Version of the Bible. Those identified as (NRSV) are taken from the New Revised Standard Version of the Bible. Those identified as (MKJV) are taken from the Modern King James Version of the Bible. Those identified as (NLT) are taken from the New Living Translation version of the Bible. Those identified as (RSV) are taken from the Revised Standard Version. Those identified as (AMP) are taken from the Amplified Bible. Those identified as (CEB) are taken from the Common English version of the Bible. Those identified as (NIV) are taken from the New International Version of the Bible. Those identified as (TWOT) are taken from the Theological Wordbook of the Old Testament.

WestBow Press books may be ordered through booksellers or by contacting:

WestBow Press
A Division of Thomas Nelson
1663 Liberty Drive
Bloomington, IN 47403
www.westbowpress.com
1-(866) 928-1240

Because of the dynamic nature of the Internet, any web addresses or links contained in this book may have changed since publication and may no longer be valid. The views expressed in this work are solely those of the author and do not necessarily reflect the views of the publisher, and the publisher hereby disclaims any responsibility for them.

Any people depicted in stock imagery provided by Thinkstock are models, and such images are being used for illustrative purposes only.

Certain stock imagery © Thinkstock.

ISBN: 978-1-4497-3952-2 (hbk)
ISBN: 978-1-4497-3951-5 (sc)
ISBN: 978-1-4497-3950-8 (e)

Library of Congress Control Number: 2012901983

Printed in the United States of America

WestBow Press rev. date: 02/20/2012

Contents

Acknowledgements ix

Preface xiii

Chapter 1: Created for Purpose 1

Chapter 2: The Thief of Purpose 29

Chapter 3: The Consequences of Misdirected Emotions 47

Chapter 4: In Pursuit of Purpose 69

Chapter 5: Called to Conquer 92

Chapter 6: The Spirit Woman 107

Chapter 7: Now Break Forth! 118

Conclusion: The Only Way to a Purposed Life 127

Afterword 131

In Memory of My Mother

This book is dedicated to the memory of my dear mother, Virginia B. Blackwell, who transitioned to her heavenly home on December 17, 2008, shortly after titling and blessing this work. Her selfless love, compassion, humility, and wisdom exemplified the nature of Christ. I thank God for this true "daughter of Zion," who was the epitome of a purposed woman, touching her family and innumerable lives with the unconditional and unfailing love and the grace of God. Today, I celebrate her life and legacy, forever mindful that she apprehended that for which she was also apprehended of Christ Jesus. One of her favorite hymns, "Precious Memories", written by J. B. F. Wright, now echoes in my heart with great meaning: "Precious memories how they linger, how they ever flood my soul, in the stillness of the midnight, precious sacred scenes unfold."

Her testimony can be conveyed through the chorus of another great hymn, "He Touched Me", written by Bill Gaither: "He touched me, He touched me, and oh the joy that floods my soul, something happened and now I know, He touched me and made me whole."

Acknowledgements

I give thanks for my awesome, wonderful, all wise, all powerful, beautiful, holy, and sovereign Lord and Savior, Jesus Christ. I think of your mercy and graciousness in my life and say as Job said in Job 42:2-6, *"I know that you can do all everything, And that no purposes of Yours can be held from you. You asked, 'Who is this who hides counsel without knowledge?' Therefore I have uttered what I did not understand, Things too wonderful for me, which I did not know. Listen, please, and let me speak;*

You said, 'I will question you, and you shall answer Me. "I have heard of You by the hearing of the ear, But now my eye sees You. Therefore I abhor myself, And repent in dust and ashes." (NKJV) Thank you for the awesome revelation that you saved my life so that I would lose it for your eternal purposes. I no longer live for this life but for the next one, which is eternity with you. It is a pleasure and privilege to know you, love you, and serve you. You are the air I breathe, and I will forever worship you.

I thank my loving and wonderful family. I thank God for each of you and the role you play in my life, growth, and development. You not only watched but prayed for me, believing that God would give me beauty for ashes, the oil of joy for mourning, and the garment of praise for the spirit of heaviness. We continually marvel over His majesty. I thank God for my four sons and one precious princess. It is a privilege to have you, serve you, and love you. Regardless of what you endure, you are called, blessed, and favored by God! I decree and declare that you will walk in health, purpose, clarity, affluence, and influence.

I thank Joseph M. Copeland (pastor emeritus, teacher, evangelist, and apostolic leader) and Lillian Copeland for your sixty-plus years of honorable marriage, faithful service to the body of Christ, and your demonstration of godly love, character, wisdom, patience, integrity, and strength. Your humility, biblical foundation, integrity, and love for God's people that I have witnessed set the standard for my life and ministry. Thank you, Pastor Copeland, for leading me into an intimate and blessed relationship with Jesus Christ, the love of my life, and remaining our family's pastor and father in the faith for more than fifty years. Your pastoral leadership and stewardship of the lives of the Blackwell family has blessed us more than you can know. In heaven you shall wear a golden crown with innumerable stars and dwell in indescribable places.

Dr. Anthony and Paula Taylor, thank you for answering the call and picking up the mantle after Joseph M. Copeland retired and for seven years of teaching, imparting and being young godly examples. Your vision and "crazy" faith, coupled with diligence and perseverance, taught me that all things are possible to those who believe. It was under your leadership that I developed the faith to believe and do that which seemed impossible. Thanks for the big PUSH! Bishop B. Courtney and Pastor Janeen McBath, in a time of recovery, your lives and ministry truly helped me to "discover life at Calvary" again and "embrace life, live life, and give life" at the next level. Under your leadership I was challenged, transformed, and enhanced in every area of life.

Finally, I could call my pastor, Dr. Geoffrey V. Guns (aka "Dad"), and his wife Rosetta Guns by many titles, but most of all, I call you friends. Beyond tradition and religion, you saw the reality of God's will in my life, and He used you to push me further into my call to serve nations. In lonely and difficult times of great loss, you taught and nurtured me in my purpose. You will never imagine how you will be rewarded by God for your role in my life. I love you more than I can say, not because of what you've done, but for who you are in the kingdom of God. You possess a love for God's people and the work of His kingdom. You promote others before yourself, and continually avail yourself to God to bless and nurture not only those in your ministry but people across the world. You are beautiful and precious gifts to the body of Christ and will be remembered forever.

Special thanks are due to the Back to the Garden Ministries volunteers, my closest friends, and co-laborers in the ministry. Thank you for your prayers, encouragement, and dedication to the work. Thank you for loving, sowing, and most of all seeing through the eyes of faith, and allowing me to be both human and supernatural. I thank God for the honor of knowing, serving, and loving you. As you very well know, this is all the Lord's doing, and it's marvelous in our eyes. Let us all continue to make the name of Jesus Christ glorious, while releasing His love and message of salvation to the world!

Preface

In order to walk effectively with God and be used by Him, we must first truly understand and embrace Him for who He is and then embrace who we are in Him. During the journey outlined in this book, you will be equipped, encouraged, and empowered to walk victoriously in God's purpose and plans for your life. You will uncover and understand the deeply rooted hindrances that impede your ability to embrace God's purpose and walk in His promises. There are things within each of us that challenge who we are in Christ, occasionally causing us to misrepresent Him. We often repeat negative behaviors and processes simply because we fail to closely examine our issues, poor decisions, misunderstandings, and the true motivations of our actions. We fail to seek God in prayer, to ask Him to expose the root of our issues so we can see ourselves accurately, and then honestly repent, which requires a true turning away from certain actions and behaviors. We plead with God, "take it out . . . help me . . . change me . . ." without being proactive and willing to do our part in the process of our renewal. There are some things that we need to surrender and release. We don't need them magically wiped away! We need to see them, sincerely repent, be healed, and "go and sin no more." The Bible declares in 2 Corinthians 7:1: "Having therefore these promises, dearly beloved, let us cleanse ourselves from all filthiness of the flesh and spirit, perfecting holiness in the fear of God" (KJV). Again, we must do our part in this process in recognition of the promise that God is our Father and we are His sons and daughters.

As you read and study these God-inspired words, you will explore deep truths that reveal your identity and purpose as a woman. You will discover who you are, why you were created, what God expects of you, how to give and receive true love and respect, and how to walk as a purposed woman in Christ. You will fully understand what the Word of God says about you as well as the many responsibilities you have as a woman in times such as these. The scriptural revelations in this book, coupled with prayer and study, will equip, encourage, and empower you to walk in the fullness of your purpose as a woman of God, operating in the Holy Spirit as a tree of life to all. You will grasp the awesomeness of God, and the power and wisdom with which He has equipped you to do His work on earth, while crushing the head (authority) of the enemy in your life and his authority over the lives of those connected to you.

In today's society, particularly in our Western culture, we are bombarded with ways to "quench the thirst" of our flesh. Women are depicted as strong and independent; yet in reality, we are often damaged and lack understanding of the purpose for which God created us. Abuse, demonic strongholds, increasingly negative influences from the media, and limited holy and victorious living examples, have left many women broken and in need of healing by the transforming power of the Holy Spirit. We profess to be purposed but often are flesh- and world-focused as we quench "our thirst," which too often is not a thirst for the things of God.

This book aims to identify and break the many societal, demonic, and self-imposed barriers that hinder women from reaching their full potential. Through God's Word, we will understand how to overcome the enemies of our soul. Instead of being led by our desires and the lust of the flesh, we will learn how to develop the disciplines that will allow us to submit to the will of God. If you embark on this journey with an open heart, you will experience the healing, peace, and freedom that will thrust you into a purposeful and victorious new life.

When we look at the powerful revelations found in the early chapters of Genesis, we learn how to overcome our three greatest enemies: the flesh, the world, and the devil. Moreover, we can understand how every attack Satan launches against us is only an opportunity to exercise our power, authority, and victory through Jesus Christ, destroy satanic ploys, and bring glory to God. It is the demonstration of God's character and nature that we should exemplify in every situation. When we realize that through Christ we have full authority over Satan, we will live a more fruitful life.

Before we explore the truths contained in this book, let us agree in prayer that we will embrace the treasures of God's Word. Let us take authority over the messages and lies that the enemy uses to fill the minds of God's people and destroy the women that He desires to set free and raise up in the earth. We bind every principality and wickedness seated in high places that seeks to deceive God's people, and we set loose the Spirit of Truth, who illuminates His Word. We release the power and anointing that comes from the Godhead. We reclaim and call forth the souls of our sisters who are burdened and deceived by the subtle yet deadly demonic suggestions that come to destroy them before they can follow the purpose of God. In Jesus's name, we cast down every imagination, idea, or thought that would be exalted against this Word. We pray further that as we embark on our transformations into genuine purposed women, we will be challenged, encouraged, and provoked to be all that God desires. We pray for a great arising of virtuous women—the wives, mothers, daughters, sisters, teachers, evangelists, pastors, apostles, prophets, community and business leaders, all the purposed women on earth—who refuse to sell out to the flesh, the world, or the devil. We believe God for the manifestation of these prayers and look forward to the life-changing testimonies that will come from the readers. In the matchless, almighty name of Jesus, who is the Christ! Amen.

Chapter 1

Created for Purpose

So God created man in his own image, in the image of God created he him, male and female created he them. (Genesis 1:27 KJV)

It is not good that the man should be alone: I will make him an help meet for him. (Genesis 2:18 KJV)

And the rib, which the Lord God had taken from the man, made he a woman, and brought her unto the man. And Adam said this is now bone of my bone and flesh of my flesh; she shall be called Woman because she was taken out of man. (Genesis 2:22, 23 KJV)

To understand the creation of woman, we must examine three key subjects associated with the topic: 1) her name, 2) her design, and 3) her purpose. We begin our study by looking into the significance of the name (and associated words) given to describe and identify the first woman.

Her Name

The Word of God clearly states that we were made in the image of God (Genesis 1:27). We not only must embrace this truth but also believe that God patterned us after Himself. These are irrefutable facts. Our difficulty with breaking through our flesh (our carnal-sin nature) causes us to fail to exemplify the characteristics, similarities, and ways of God, which in turn makes it difficult to grasp the idea that we are made in His image.

To understand who we are as women, we look first to Genesis 2:18 and the word God used to name His creation. *Merriam-Webster's Dictionary* defines *name* as "a title or word by which someone or something is known." The King James Version (KJV) of the Bible refers to the woman as a *help meet*. The New International Version (NIV) version translates *help meet* as "a helper suitable."

The Hebrew word for helper is *azar*, which according to the Strong's Concordance means "to help, support, aid, or protect." Dr. David Eckman writes in his online article, Back to Eden, God Formed the Man and Fashioned the Woman:

> God paid a compliment to women with this word. The same word is used in Psalm 115:9, where it states, "O Israel, trust in the Lord, for He is their Helper and shield" (KJV). The term is always used to describe someone who brings significant help and someone who delivers another from some great dilemma. When the ancient Hebrew speaking Israelite heard the term used to describe Eve, he would have been impressed. He would have thought of women, therefore, as a God-like gift from God.

In several passages in the New Testament, *helper* is used to describe the Holy Spirit. In many of those verses, the Greek text uses *ezer* as the translation for both woman and the Holy Spirit. Throughout Scripture, many of the characteristics attributed to women parallel those of the Holy Spirit. The Holy Spirit is our *paraclete*—our protector, the support on which we lean for guidance, and the one who leads us into all truth. *Paraclete* is a Greek noun that means "comforter" or "advocate."

Paraclete can also mean "a calling to one's side" or "one who comes alongside." Proverbs 31:11-12 shows this aspect of being a help meet: "The heart of her husband doth safely trust in her, so that he shall have no need of spoil. She will do him good and not evil all the days of her life" (KJV). This speaks to the assisting, comforting, and supportive, life-giving qualities found in women, qualities that mirror those of the Holy Spirit.

When in operation, these godly qualities influence the lives of a woman's family, friends, and all with whom she interacts. The positive influence of women is so powerful, the enemy often uses their mistreatment and abuse as a tool for releasing adverse effects on the quality and quantity of life released through women. This causes a continuation of damage and scars throughout generations. Using brokenness and deficiencies in women is one of the enemy's greatest strategies for robbing this generation, by preventing them from receiving the treasures released through healthy, godly women.

In addition to naming woman a help meet, God said that she would be suitable for that role. *Merriam-Webster's Dictionary* defines *suitable* as "comparable or equivalent to; to meet the requirements of; or sound mentally and physically." *Comparable* is defined as "capable of or suitable for comparison; similar, like." Again, we see the connection between *suitable* or *comparable* and being a helper. God created woman to be a suitable or comparable helper to man. She was made his equal; however, she was given a protective and supportive quality to provide the necessary assistance and balance to the man in his roles, responsibilities, and purposes on earth.

If you were looking for someone to help you, would you want someone weak or strong? You would seek the most well-equipped person you could find! It was no different when God formed the helper for Adam. He attended to the details, creating her with the strength she needed to help Adam perform the task set before him. As much as the world minimizes the role of the helper, it is a powerful, important, and necessary role that drives our purpose as women. The role denotes strength, wisdom, and influence.

We must understand the value of our role as women. We were created with great intention and purpose. We have great influence, and in that influence is the power to help or hurt, to give life or death, and to heal or break with our words, actions, and attitudes. Understanding the way and the reason we were created is an essential part of becoming a truly purposed woman.

Purposeful Thoughts

How often have you, like Eve, known what you were supposed to do but failed to do it? We often have *knowledge* that is void of *understanding* and *wisdom*. Such knowledge can cause us to function improperly in our roles as women.

Interestingly enough, in Eve's calling to help Adam, bringing him fruit would have been considered great help. However, once Eve entered into discussion with the Devil, her desires, lusts, and emotions were aroused, making her help deadly . . . literally.

It's not enough to know what to do. We must do it! The Bible instructs us in James 1:22 to be not only hearers of God's Word but also doers. In order to be true helpers, we must crucify our flesh and its deadly desires. Let's go beyond knowledge and seek God's wisdom and understanding. The Word declares:

> Get wisdom! Get understanding! Do not forget, nor turn away from the words of my mouth. Do not forsake her, and she will preserve you; love her, and she will keep you. Wisdom is the principal thing; therefore get wisdom. And in all your getting, get understanding. Exalt her, and she will promote you; she will bring you honor, when you embrace her. She will place on your head an ornament of grace; A crown of glory she will deliver to you." (Proverbs 4:5-9 NKJV)

Operating in the wisdom and understanding obtained through Christ will help us function properly as women of purpose, as those who are called "suitable helpers." Wisdom will help us to know what we are to do, while understanding will help us submit to the knowledge we have gained. Let us pursue the priceless asset of wisdom before we act. The Bible states in James 1:5 that if we lack wisdom, we may ask of God and He will give it freely, holding none back. Ask, and ye shall receive! In the devotional notes below note the areas in which you could use more wisdom and understanding in your daily life. Trust God to freely release it to you. During your time of reading, use the devotional notes throughout this book to address the things that come to mind as you read the transformational truths necessary for purposeful living in this book.

Devotional Notes

Let's examine a verse from Scripture that is often misunderstood and sometimes taken out of context. First Peter 3:7 reads, "Likewise, ye husbands, dwell with them according to knowledge, giving honor unto the wife as unto the weaker vessel, and as being heirs together of the grace of life; that your prayers be not hindered" (KJV). In this Scripture, Peter is *not* referring to the spiritual, emotional, or mental state of women when he refers to them as "weaker." Rather, he is instructing men to recognize and protect women because of their weaker physical frames, which often makes them the target of attack, abuse, and mistreatment.

When Peter tells men to "dwell with [women] according to knowledge," he means that men should have an understanding of what women have to face, and accordingly to deal with them with honor, respect, love, and kindness. Note that Peter also includes a warning: "that your prayers be not hindered." Simply stated, to directly disobey these instructions could cause a husband's prayers to remain unanswered. We must have a true understanding of the Scriptures to effectively live and convey the word of God to others. It is important to know that God doesn't see women as broken or meaningless. He sees you as valuable, and His desire is that you be honored, loved, and protected as an equal heir because of your importance in His kingdom.

Woman of God, there is a purpose for your life. You are a suitable helper, designed to enhance the lives of those you influence. Whether you know it or not, people are watching you, and their success, or lack of it, could easily be dependent upon you. What will you show them? On the path to purpose, embrace the truth that God made you suitable and valuable!

Release life!

Hope D. Blackwell

Questions

1) In what ways can you become a more suitable helper in various areas of your life?

2) How can these characteristics be a blessing to those in your sphere of influence?

Let us further study the truths revealed by the name given to the first woman. The name *Eve* means "giver of life." Of course we know that to be appropriate, as she was the first mother recorded in Scripture. However, her name meant more than "life giver" in the obvious sense of the word. Eve's name was a foreshadowing of what was to come, that women would be givers of life through their influence in every area.

God is calling us to be the helpers, protectors, and women of wisdom who will release life, not only to our spouses, families, and others but also into their situations, visions, and ideas. We must also release life into our own spirit, encouraging ourselves at times when our flesh (our carnal-sin nature) is strong and overpowering, and needs to be subjected to the Holy Spirit and the word of God.

The Bible states that "she is a tree of life to them who lay hold upon her: and happy is every one that retaineth her" (Proverbs 3:18 KJV). God expects us to be women who release life, even though at times it seems that life is being drained from us. We must ask ourselves, "Are we giving life to anyone? When people leave our presence, have they received hope in their situation? Have life's difficult circumstances caused us to become callous women without compassion or love?"

We must be discerning enough to know when to be assertive and when to minister with the grace, love, and compassion of Christ. The Word of God describes occasions when Jesus was frustrated with foolish and faithless behavior. However, He continued to minister with patience, love, and compassion. Jesus always walked in healthy balance, providing the example we are to follow. He had such ability to release truth and life! He could destroy a negative word or demonic spirit and give life, all in one statement. If we are discerning, wise, and led by the Spirit of God, we, too, can communicate effectively as He did.

Eve's name reveals another life-changing truth, revealed at the moment her name was introduced in Scripture: Genesis 3:20, where she was also called "the mother of all living." Interestingly enough, Adam called her the mother of all living before she gave birth to their firstborn but after God's judgment upon them. Adam called her Eve not based only on the natural meaning of her name but on who she was. He demonstrated the wisdom and authority that he used when he named the animals. With that God-given insight, he understood her purpose to be a life giver, despite the fact that she had not yet given birth, and had introduced them both to death by taking and sharing the forbidden fruit. Despite the circumstances, he understood her purpose as a life giver, and named her as such.

Eve's name is mentioned next in Genesis 4:1, which describes the couple's intimate relations that will lead to the conception and birth of their son. Note that Eve had been previously referred to as "woman", until these two verses. Did you know that intimacy is a defining moment in the life of a woman, which is one of many reasons that God calls us to intimacy only in marriage with one husband? It is a truth that we are identified by those with whom we become intimate. Many of us have been labeled based on our decisions to become intimate with the wrong people, places, and things—i.e., physical, emotional, and spiritual intimacies. This has left many women striving to find themselves after being scarred by such relations. *Merriam-Webster's* defines *intimacy* as "a close and personal association with someone and/or something." Whenever there is intimacy, something is produced. We must be cautious about whom we entertain, associate, or become intimate. We want to be givers of life, producing spiritually life-giving seed. We do not want to produce seeds of lust, confusion, or discord, which lead to death, because of incorrect affiliations. Those entanglements will hinder the fulfillment of purpose and could abort God's wonderful plan for our lives as well as the lives of others. Too often those associations are rooted in motives that are based in desire, flesh, ambition, personal gain, and deceptions. God is calling us to be identified based on who we are in Him, where our lives bear witness to that identification.

Purposeful Thoughts

Have you allowed negative associations, relationships, or damaging connections to hinder you from walking in the perfect will of God? Take an honest assessment of your relationships and note those that are questionable. Do they lack purpose? Will they ultimately strengthen you or bring God glory? What fruit is being produced from these relationships? What kind of preventative measures can you take to avoid entering into ungodly connections? Seek after the relationships God desires, those that are a part of His plan and purpose for your life. The Bible declares in John 8:32 that we should know the truth, and the truth shall make us free. Be free as you wholeheartedly abolish all ungodly ties as well as the influences they have over your life. God wants to set you free and make you a giver of pure life!

Devotional Notes

Questions

1) Considering the life-giving characteristics placed in you by God, what are some dead areas in or around you or those you influence that you can release life into?

2) What are the unhealthy physical, emotional, or spiritual bonds that may be producing the wrong fruit in your life? What can you do to break away from those people, places, and things?

Too often we allow the voices of others, the enemy, and even our very own self-destructive thoughts and imaginations to alter our "name." We receive words from and are influenced by those who God has not called to speak, and as a result our lives are affected in various ways. No matter what others have named you, today God calls you His precious daughter. He knows your name, and if you need a name and character change, He is more than able. I am reminded of how He changed the name of Jacob, which means one who deceives, to the name Israel, which means a prince who prevails with God and man. The Bible says that Jacob wrestled all night with the angel, making supplication for the blessing of transformation. The angel seemed to resist his prayer and at the same time endeavored to break away from him, but admirably Jacob insisted on holding the angel, not just by using physical strength, but by the power of living faith. In this time of distress and reflection, Jacob referred to the repentance of his soul, the deep humility he felt, and his relentless desire to be free from the pain and daunting of his past demons. Jacob prevailed and the course of his life was changed; he received divine intervention in every area that concerned him.

Dear friend, God called you not only a helper, but a suitable helper, the mother of all living, and in His Word He also declares that you have been fearfully and wonderfully made. I thank God for your life and for creating, calling, and naming you for such a time as this. I declare you are becoming a purposed woman!

Her Design

After reviewing the area of study concerning "Her Name", now let us review Genesis 2:22, 23 and explore the study centered around "Her Design", which is the way in which she was formed. This will also further validate our study of the helper and her life-giving attributes.

As detailed in Scripture, the woman was fashioned from the rib, which was taken out of the man. Let's examine the significance of the rib. According to Wikipedia, "the ribs are the long curved bones surrounding the chest, enabling the lungs to expand and thus facilitate breathing by expanding the chest cavity. They serve to protect the lungs, heart, and other internal organs of the thorax". Clearly, *one of the rib's major functions is to provide the protection that will assist in keeping the body operating in health.* This validates the protective quality intended in the woman's design. This rib is one of the strongest bones in the body, yet it also is one of the most delicately designed. Interestingly enough, it also has the flexibility to expand and contract for the purposes of the body's essential need to breathe. An injured or damaged rib has an adverse effect on the entire body, making it almost impossible to function; in extreme cases, it can cause death. If the rib breaks due to severe damage or blunt force, it could subsequently pierce the very organs that it was originally designed to protect. This presents a deadly situation, which I call a "rib puncture." Because if the rib is broken, it no longer wraps around and protects what is vital in the body; instead, the broken rib pierces and punctures the body. Women of God, we must embrace this powerful revelation of the rib.

We have been formed so delicately and uniquely, yet with the strength to fulfill the great and awesome privilege of being a helper and protector. We must understand that, like the rib, we have been called to shield, wrap around, and protect others. However, we must remain flexible enough to provide freedom to function. There are times when the blows of life and the consequences of decisions damage and break us. If we remain broken and unhealed, we will become a deadly vice to the people and things we are designed to protect and support. How often have you started out with the best intentions, but through some misunderstanding, offense, or abuse turned into a source of pain instead? (In a sense, you have become a "rib puncture.") How about the woman that seems to have your best interests at heart, but resorts to cursing you in the heat of the moment? The supportive and protective quality within us is a gift from God, but we must learn to manage that gift properly and be led by the Spirit. We must not be led by our emotions, frustrations, desires, and lusts. We must stop and determine who or what we are really fighting for or protecting, in light of God's directions and desires.

Many times, because of brokenness, distrust, or scars from the past, we are so busy trying to protect and fight for ourselves that we fail to focus on our spouses, family, or brothers and sisters in Christ. We must recognize our selfish tendencies, and choose to be like Christ. The Bible says in Philippians 2:5-8:

> Let this mind be in you, which was also in Christ Jesus: Who, being in the form of God, thought it not robbery to

be equal with God: but made himself of no reputation, and took upon him the form of a servant, and was made in the likeness of men; and being found in fashion as a man, he humbled himself, and became obedient unto death. (KJV)

Questions

1) In what ways are you demonstrating your rib-like (supportive, protective, encasing) qualities in your home, marriage, marketplace, and community?

2) Often "rib punctures" occur when in a high emotional state. If you look closely at the times that you have "spazzed out" and "misfired," what emotion was at its peak? Were you angry, hurt, disappointed, sad, lonely, unheard, or unappreciated? Identify that emotion, and make a covenant to take authority over it whenever it rises within. Avoid being driven to operate in a broken state.

Purposeful Thoughts

On your purposeful journey, ask God for healing and strength. Moreover, ask Him for the wisdom to prevent further breakages or damage in your life. God loves you, and He is the perfect doctor. He'll not only heal the break, He'll make it look like it never happened. If you ask, He'll show you the x-ray of where and when the damage began, and how He healed that too! I am a woman who didn't always live a purposed life. I can remember numerous breaks, damage, and pains from as far back as my childhood and even those that occurred later in my adult life. As I consider my many mistakes and "rib punctures," I bless God because He ushered me on a purposeful journey, exposed those problem areas, and ministered understanding, healing, and grace that afforded me the opportunity to walk in health! Think about some of the breaks that have caused your "rib punctures," and ask God to show you the x-rays. Make your "devotional notes" in the space below, and list the things that God shows you as current and potential issues. Get the preventative maintenance plan, found in the Word of God and make a commitment to walk in His prescribed purpose for your life, which I guarantee will lead you to victory and success.

Devotional Notes

Let's further study the truth exposed through this typical scenario:

> You believe you are helping your husband or another individual be a better person when you "share" your feelings, opinions, and ideas. Because the other person may not agree with you, fail to change, or respond in a different way than you expected, you resort to nagging, complaining, and fussing about his or her poor communication, lack of understanding, and childish behavior. You are still communicating, but from a bruised condition. Instead of protecting, supporting, and nurturing, you are inflicting unwarranted injury, pain, and damage. In this case, you must carefully examine yourself. Who and what are you really trying to protect? What would God say about your actions and motives? How can you become a life giver?

When pain and frustration cause our feelings and emotions to rise within us, at that point we should stop "helping" or "ministering" to the individual. At that point, we have ceased to be helpers and have become the ones who need correction, change, and healing. Whenever we feel our last nerve has been plucked, we must temporarily cease all attempts to be the helper and supporter. In actuality, we have become a snare, causing damage to the individual and the relationship. We allow ourselves to abandon our purpose when we do not get the response that we want, and resort to operating in the flesh (carnal-sin nature), which causes us to shift from building up to tearing down. In these situations, we should truthfully address our feelings, repent, and ask God to give us the wisdom, patience, and strength we need to respond in a life giving manner even in difficult times.

There is a prophetic anointing on women to speak and extend life. As with any authority, when misused or manipulated, it can have devastating effects. The Bible declares in Proverbs 12:4: "a virtuous woman is a crown to her husband, but she that maketh him ashamed is like rottenness to his bones" (KJV). This Scripture compares the woman to a crown. A crown is worn on the head, and according to the Easton's Bible Dictionary the biblical meaning is "to encircle for attack or protection, to compass.", taken from the Hebrew word "atarah", meaning circlet. Most head coverings are designed to enhance, surround, or protect the head. The Hebrew word for "virtuous" is a translation of the Hebrew "chavil" (or "havil"). According to the Theological Wordbook of the Old Testament "chavil" is used to denote "strength, power, or might" in a variety of ways. It may refer to the strength of God (Ps. 59:11), the physical strength of man (Eccl. 10:10), or even the strength of a plant (Joel 2:22). And, according to Young's Analytical Concordance, "chavil" is translated "valor" 37 times and translated "army" 54 times.

"When used of a woman (Ruth 3:11; Prov. 12:4; 31:10) it is translated 'virtuous', but it may well be that a woman of this caliber had all the attributes of her male counterpart" (TWOT). The masculine attributes described seem to indicate an individual not only with physical strength, but also strength of character, and possibly one of some wealth and social standing. And the attributes of the "virtuous" woman as shown in Proverbs 31 seem to fit that pattern.

The Scripture reveals that the woman who is prepared to enhance, encircle, and do warfare as an army on behalf of her husband and family is a crown, but she who is not is like a cancer or subtle destroyer. The Bible teaches us that the husband is the head of the wife; however, many misunderstand this Scripture and, as a result, minimize the authority, influence, and power given to women. Interestingly enough, the Scriptures further validate and define our design and purpose as women. When walking in purpose, we can envelop those we love, as we enhance, protect, and support them, making them shine. Woman of God, this is what crowns were designed to do!

Consider how often our emotions, mind, and will, when not subject to the Holy Spirit, will cause us to become opinionated, unforgiving, aggressive, critical, uptight, moody, and quite unChristlike! We quickly speak our opinions and set unrealistic standards for others, but often are unwilling to live up to them ourselves. This encourages us to become arrogant, proud, judgmental, and ultimately sabotage our relationships. Women who possess these characteristics fail to bring joy to their environments, much less peace. In reality, they produce drought rather than releasing the living waters that the Word of God speaks about. This is the dryness that breeds a place for demonic infiltration, the dryness that demons seek when trying to find a dwelling place. I believe it is also the rottenness that is referred to in Proverbs 12:4. The Word of God tells us it is better to dwell on the rooftop than with a brawling or confrontational woman. Have you checked your roof lately?

Women of God, we must press toward the prize that is the higher calling in Christ Jesus, and crucify our flesh. We must recognize our life-giving attributes as a gift, while understanding there is a price for operating in the fullness of this call, i.e., death to the flesh! I often say, *Jesus died so we could have life, and now we must die so He can live in and through us!* The sooner we die, the sooner we release life. Paul teaches that those who live according to the flesh set their minds on what the flesh desires, but those who live according to the Spirit set their minds on what the Spirit desires. To be spiritually minded is life and peace (Romans 8:5-6 NIV). We must stay spiritually minded by continuing in God's Word and the Holy Spirit, so that we become the protectors, support systems, and life givers we were created to be. How can you become more spiritually minded and filled with more life and peace to release and share with those around you? Note areas in your life where you may need transformation.

Questions

1) What are some ways that you can exercise your ability to speak and extend life in your marriage, family, community, business, or ministry?

2) What are areas of your flesh that may be blocking you from releasing life into others?

Devotional Notes

Her Purpose

As we study the third and final area necessary for understanding the way in which woman was created, we will define and analyze the difference between identity and purpose. *Identity* is who we are, how we are defined. *Merriam-Webster's* defines *identity* as "the distinguishing character or personality of an individual." Though identity and purpose are not interchangeable, one does not operate independent of the other. Identity can help or hinder the fulfillment of purpose. *Vine's Complete Expository Dictionary of Old and New Testament Words* lists one of the common Hebrew interpretations for purpose as *protithemae*, which means "a setting forth or to have set before." The Greek word for purpose is *gnome*, which means "to be, to become, or an expected end." Purpose is defined by *Merriam-Webster's* as "something set up as an object or end to be."

An interesting fact about purpose is that it is fully revealed in time. Identity, in some form, is established and seen; it's recognizable and seen in the natural. However, God's purpose is revealed through time, prayer, intimacy with Him through Jesus Christ, and obedience to His commands. You can be identified by both God and man, but those identifications will differ greatly. Man and God look at totally different traits and characteristics. According to 1 Samuel 16, when sent to anoint God's choice for the next king, even the prophet Samuel was about to make the selection according to identity rather than God's purpose and destiny. The Bible declares in 1 Samuel 16:6-8: "So it was, when they came, that he looked at Eliab and said, 'Surely the Lord's anointed is before Him!' But the Lord said to Samuel, 'Do not look at his appearance or at his physical stature, because I have refused him. For the Lord does not see as man sees; for man looks at the outward appearance, but the Lord looks at the heart'" (ESV).

As individuals, we often assume false identities. With prayer, the people we truly are eventually will be revealed, and hopefully transformed, if necessary. However, purpose is realized and achieved through time, growth, and intimacy with God. Purpose is established by God; it is not based upon what man sees or feels, but what God knows. Jeremiah 29:11 states: "I know the thoughts that I think toward you, saith the Lord, thoughts of peace and not of evil, to give you an expected end" (KJV). The NIV version of the same passage is, "I know the plans I have for you, plans to prosper you and not to harm you, plans to give you hope and a future." God knew everything about us long before we were ever born. He knows our every deed, conversation, choice, gifting, and calling. It is the will of God for you to know His purpose for your life and pursue it. Your current identity may not look like it has a good ending, but it can have a godly ending if you embrace Him and His plans. Furthermore, you are in good company because things didn't look favorable in various stages of the lives of Paul, Esther, Peter, Ruth, Naomi, David, Jacob, Joseph and many other great people in the Bible. God's Word instructs us that many are the plans of man, but the counsel of the Almighty shall stand.

Satan often attempts to release demonic strategies and ploys to cause us to forsake or lose faith in the truth of God's Word, but he has no authority or power over purpose. Often, we allow the blows of life, poor decision-making, and Satan's schemes to plunge us into a hole of depression and hopelessness, after which comes the pity party. We may follow that course, not realizing there are certain things God has allowed Satan to do, things that will actually thrust us into the purpose God has for us, if we do not submit and give in to the ploys and tactics of the enemy. (Consider the accounts of Job.) Anything that Satan does concerning us must be approved by God, which once again affirms the limitations of Satan's power and proves that God is in full control. He has plans of good, not evil, that will lead to His expected end for us.

> One day the angels came to present themselves to the Lord and Satan also came with them. The Lord said to Satan, "Where have you come from?" Satan answered the Lord, "From roaming the earth going back and forth in it." The Lord said to Satan, "Have you considered my servant Job? There is no one on earth like him; he is blameless and upright, a man who fears God and shuns evil." (Job 1:6-8 NIV)

This conversation between Satan and the Lord reveals the limited influence Satan has over God's people. In the last chapter of Job is one of the verses of Scripture that I treasure. It is the part when Job finally replies to the Lord concerning the orchestration of his life. He says, "I know that you can do all things; no plan of yours can be thwarted. Surely I spoke of things I did not understand, things to wonderful for me to know . . . My ears had heard of you but now my eyes have seen you" (Job 42:1-6 NIV). This is a beautiful declaration from Job, who understands that with all the horrible things that have occurred in his life—the trauma, pain, loss, physical detriment, accusations, and heartaches—God is forming something that is too wonderful for him to fathom. He declares that surely he knew of God, but after those things he has seen Him in all His power and splendor! The book concludes with the blessings that God lavishes on Job. The latter part of Job's life has more blessings than the former. Job's life is a testimony of God's omnipotence, sovereignty, uncommon ways, and wisdom. We understand how God's magnificent plan unfolds, and His intent to bless and prosper Job comes to pass, as Job continues to walk in his purposed life as a man of God, in faith. In the end, he sees the greater glory of God in his life.

So often, like Job, we cannot understand or even imagine why God would allow certain things to occur in our lives, particularly as "women on a purposed journey." As Christians, we pray and cry out to God, "not my will, but thy will," and "use me, Lord." But when adversity comes, we are quick to rebuke the assignment, without considering that it could be a God-approved and God-ordained test or challenge that is His will and perhaps preparation for a much grander picture that will bring glory to God. In the process of our faith and diligence, He will be glorified, and we will receive His richest blessings and rewards if we "faint not." Our faith sometimes wanes, and we forget the awesomeness and sovereignty of God. We must realistically attend to our human part but learn to quickly resort to the mindset of Job: "Naked I came from my mother's womb and naked I will depart. The Lord giveth and the Lord has taken away; may the name of the Lord be praised" (Job 1:20-22 NIV). In the midst of it all, Job was saying that despite everything that was transpiring in his life, the name of the Lord was worthy of praise! Job was not calling out the name of God because of what he had or understood. He probably didn't understand much at that time. No, he worshipped God for His sovereignty. In the end, Job's outward identity before men was transformed to line up with his God-ordained destiny, proving that identity can often look contrary to destiny, but in the hands of God, it is beautified.

Purposeful Thoughts

> The book of Ecclesiastes states, "there is a time for every purpose under Heaven" (3:1 NKJV). Ecclesiastes goes on to say that God has made everything beautiful in its time. Also, He has put eternity in their hearts, except that no one can find out the work that God does from beginning to end. I know that nothing is better for them than to rejoice, and to do good in their lives, and also that every man should eat and drink and enjoy the good of all his labor, it is the gift of God. I know that whatever God does, it shall be forever. Nothing can be added to it, And nothing taken from it. God does it that men should fear before Him. That which is has already been, and what is to be has already been; and God requires an account of what is past. (Ecclesiastes 3:11-15 NKJV)

Friend, our God is sovereign and just. Let us walk in our new identity in Christ. Don't be fooled by the enemy, or even by your own ideas, fears, or insecurities. If you do, you will surely miss your destiny and eternal rewards. At the set time, we all will have to give an account of whether we were identified by this world or found our identities in Christ. One day, we must answer the question, did we pursue our God-ordained and established destinies, or our own? What is your identity? What is your destiny? Will you allow your identity to be lined up with His destiny for your life?

Questions

1) Reflect on situations, circumstances, or thoughts that may be pulling you away from, rather than preparing you for, purpose. What does God's Word say about these things? What can you do about it?

2) What things have been Satan's direct attempts to hijack your destiny? What things have been self-imposed? Come into agreement with God about His purpose and destiny for you, and see yourself victorious over every attempt of the enemy to frustrate those plans and God's promises for your life!

Isaiah 54:16 states, "Behold, I have created the smith that bloweth the coals in the fire and that bringeth forth an instrument for his work: and I have created the waster to destroy" (KJV). The NIV version ends with "and it is I who have created the destroyer to work havoc." Remember that the enemy's job is to destroy waste by working havoc in your life. Many things in our lives are of no use to God. Simply put, they are waste. That is the only thing God permits the enemy to destroy. Satan cannot destroy us or pluck us out of the hand of God, unless we yield to him or the desires of our flesh. Remember that Isaiah 54:17 declares that "no weapon formed against you will prosper" (NKJV).

Ultimately, every trial and test helps us reach our potential and purpose. In these instances of adversities and attacks, we must lose our sorrow and shame, and allow God's perfect work to be accomplished. Too often, we are concerned with and consumed by many of the small things in life that do not advance God's purpose. We would probably be stunned at the number of things we do or say that are not inspired by or even important to God. He desires for us to prosper and be in good health—physically, emotionally, and spiritually. We must eliminate absolutely everything within us and in our lives that hinders His purpose. Remember, purpose is established by God. The enemy cannot change or alter our God-ordained purpose. He cannot attack us without permission or release. I must reiterate this point: Satan does many things to hinder our fulfillment of purpose. However, and I stress this point, anything God permits Satan to do in our lives is intended for His glory and our elevation in Him in this life and for eternity. God knows the outcome of these situations, and we must live holy and blameless lives, totally trusting Him. Actually, when take advantage of Satan's attempts to defeat us, they will destroy the flesh, which is useless for God's purpose and glory. Satan's ploys, once understood and overcome, can only better equip us to do God's will, operate in a greater anointing, and receive God's blessings, taking us from glory to glory, higher and higher. This is what God means when He speaks of making our enemies our footstool.

Making decisions apart from God's instructions can take us off the course that leads to purpose. This is when we deviate from being purposed women. In other words, we are pushing our own purpose rather than following His! There are often occurrences in our lives that are not a part of our plans; however, they may be a part of God's plan for us. In Proverbs 16:1, we find these words: "to a man belongs the plan of the heart but from the Lord comes the reply of the tongue" (NIV). As Christian women, we need to seek God in all things and rely on His omnipotence and omniscience. When we fail to see God's hand in situations and circumstances, we sometimes react swiftly and out of sync with God's will. We do this because we put Him in what I call a "God box." This happens when our failure to understand His ways causes us to limit Him to our ways and understanding. When you box Him in, you actually box yourself in, and when you finally release Him, you are released. Ah.

Think back. How often have you seen a glorious ending happen to something that had an unstable or uncertain beginning? Don't limit God. Remember, He always has a purpose and plan, and there is nothing that takes Him by surprise. According to Romans 8:28, we know that all things work together for good to those who love God, to those who are the called according to *His* purpose (NKJV). Continue to love God and embrace His purpose for your life.

Devotional Notes

To walk in the fullness of God, we must understand and accept that God is the sovereign Lord of all, and His providence is limitless. Proverbs 19:21 states, "many are the plans of a man's heart but the purpose of the Lord shall prevail" (NIV). This is a powerful testament to the sovereignty of our God. For too long, we have put God "in a box." Who are we to propose to know the plans of God? Isaiah 55:8 states, "for my thoughts are not your thoughts neither are your ways my ways", declares the Lord (NIV). Even those who think they've "got it" often discover they've missed it. Why do we need to know everything? For example, God didn't want Eve to know evil, only good, but she desired to know what God was protecting her from. Sometimes we have to believe, wait, and watch. It's natural to feel the need to "help God," but be assured, He has it all under control.

Questions

Have you misunderstood situations in your life or missed out on God's blessings because of your own limited perception or understanding? How often have you put God in a "box" and minimized your possibilities because you didn't think God would do it that way? Sound silly? We can too easily fall prey to that kind of thinking. Reflect on situations, circumstances, or even limitations in your thoughts that may have obstructed your view of God and His abilities. Write them down. These may be the very things that God has been using to usher you into purpose. How can these things be used so that God may be glorified?

To understand purpose as it relates to the creation of woman, we will explore the virtue of wisdom. A woman's success in pursuing purpose is directly linked to her ability to walk in wisdom. Throughout Scripture, wisdom is portrayed with a woman's characteristics. When God's Word speaks of wisdom, the references are to the female gender. Let's study several passages that illustrate these comparisons.

Proverbs 31:10 states, "Who can find a virtuous woman? For her price is far above rubies" (KJV). God is clearly speaking of the virtuous woman who is described in detail in this chapter. Proverbs 3:13-15 declares, "Happy is the man that findeth wisdom, and the man that getteth understanding for the merchandise of it is better than the merchandise of silver and the gain thereof than fine gold. She is more precious than rubies: and all the things thou canst desire are not to be compared to her" (KJV). Proverbs 31:25 is clearly about the woman of noble character: "strength and honor are her clothing; and she shall rejoice in the time to come" (KJV). Proverbs 3:16 reads, "Length of days is in her right hand: and in her left hand riches and honor" (KJV). In regard to wisdom, Proverbs 4:6-10 states:

> Forsake her not and she shall preserve thee: love her and she shall keep thee. Wisdom is the principal thing; therefore get wisdom and with all thy getting, get understanding. Exalt her and she shall promote thee: she shall bring thee to honor, when thou dost embrace her. She shall give to thine head an ornament of grace: a crown of glory shall she deliver to thee. (KJV)

God is clearly speaking about wisdom in this scripture. Consider, however, what He says in Proverbs 12:4: "a virtuous woman is a crown to her husband; but she that maketh ashamed is as rottenness in his bones" (KJV). Again, we see a parallel between the characteristics of woman and those of wisdom. The only other thing God references when talking about wisdom is rubies, which also indicates a woman. Proverbs 31:10 asks, "Who can find a virtuous woman? For her price is far above rubies." Again, the scripture confirms that this is a virtuous and wise woman.

I do not believe in biblical coincidence. Everything God says and does has purpose. <u>When God places emphasis on a specific thing in His Word, it requires our attention.</u> We were created by the wisdom of God to do great and mighty things. We must remember that God formed Adam, but He made Eve. Adam was a "form" that needed to be "filled in" or "fulfilled." Genesis 2:7 teaches us that Adam was formed from the dust of the ground. According to Merriam-Webster, to form means to create shape, definition, or the structure of something as distinguished from its material. Genesis 2:22 states, "The Lord made a woman from the rib He took out of the man and then brought her to the man" (NIV). The word *make* is defined by Merriam-Webster as "to assemble or set alight the materials for, or to put together from components." The fact that Eve was made by God means that He deposited into her what He knew she needed to bring fulfillment to the form of Adam. This verse from Scripture reveals that wisdom was present when God made Eve.

Proverbs 8:22-31 declares:

> The Lord brought me forth as the first of his works, before his deeds of old; I was appointed from eternity, from the beginning, before the world began. When there were no oceans, I was given birth, when there were no springs abounding with water; before the mountains were settled in place, before the hills, I was given birth, before he made the earth or its fields or any dust of the world. I was there when he set the heavens in place, when he marked out the horizon on the face of the deep, when he established the clouds above and fixed securely the fountains of the deep . . . then I was the craftsman at his side. I was filled with delight day after day, rejoicing always in his presence, rejoicing in his world and delighting in mankind. (NIV)

Wisdom is one of God's characteristics, and since we were made in His image and likeness when we become saved from a sinful life, that wisdom is available to us. We must seek God for wisdom and understanding. Proverbs 4:7 declares that wisdom is the principal thing for us to achieve, and James 1:5 lets us know that we can ask God for it, and He will freely give it to us.

Let us review another awesome revelation found in Proverbs 8:1-14:

> Does not wisdom cry out, And understanding lift up her voice? She takes her stand on the top of the high hill, beside the way, where the paths meet. She cries out by the gates, at the entry of the city, at the entrance of the doors: "To you, O men, I call, and my voice is to the sons of men. O you simple ones, understand prudence, and you fools, be of an understanding heart. Listen, for I will speak of excellent things, and from the opening of my lips will come right things; for my mouth will speak truth; Wickedness is an abomination to my lips. All the words of my mouth are with righteousness; nothing crooked or perverse is in them. They are all plain to him who understands, and right to those who find knowledge. Receive my instruction, and not silver, and knowledge rather than choice gold; for wisdom is better than rubies, and all the things one may desire cannot be compared with her. I, wisdom, dwell with prudence, and find out knowledge and discretion. The fear of the Lord is to hate evil; pride and arrogance and the evil way and the perverse mouth I hate. Counsel is mine, and sound wisdom; I am understanding, I have strength." (NKJV)

This Scripture is evidence that God has called women to arise in wisdom and strength, walking in their roles as helpers in every arena of life, having a voice in the home, community, and the world. When you look at this powerful revelation, you find that a woman who walks with the characteristics of wisdom positions herself in the most strategic and influential places (Proverbs 8:2, 3). She plainly preaches truth to all who will hear her (Proverbs 8:4-9). She recognizes and shares the value of God's wisdom, understanding that only the wisdom that comes from God possesses this indescribable value (Proverbs 8:10-12). She despises wickedness and refuses to engage in offensive and ungodly speech or practices because of her reverence for God and His wisdom, recognizing the great rewards of its possession (Proverbs 8:12-14). This is a powerful text that challenges us to act wisely. God has called us to mirror this beautiful image, personified as a woman of godly character and strength.

In studying the woman described in Proverbs 31, the model of a godly woman, we find that she not only walked in wisdom, she assisted her husband by managing the household and the businesses, while ministering to those in need, sharing with her maidens, exhibiting a meek, humble, and giving heart, and not being poisoned by the worldly systems of the marketplace. The chapter further states that her husband sat among the elders inside the city, and he praised her also. Wow, what a woman! The modern woman complains if her husband forgets to take out the trash. And yet this woman managed the affairs of her home and business, pleased her husband, shared with others, and taught her children in the process. I believe we take the tradition of men being the head of the household to unhealthy and unbiblical extremes. We put a heavy weight on the shoulders of men, not realizing that balance is necessary through the uniting of man and woman. Although the husband is the head of the wife and a leader in the family, that doesn't mean that he has to lead every aspect of the entire home and be solely responsible for its affairs and management. The Bible does not state that in any case. I believe this unhealthy imbalance of responsibility is physically, emotionally, and mentally breaking many men, who have taken on much more than God ever intended, and causes women to operate out of sync with God's plan. Imagine if the husband of the virtuous woman did everything the Bible states that she did. He surely wouldn't have been able to address the matters of the people and the community. This is why we must know how and why we were created, and walk in the healthy balance that produces the fruitfulness and multiplication that God intended!

God requires us as women to walk in wisdom. Collectively and individually, we have an awesome purpose that is linked to many facets of the kingdom of God. To effectively walk in purpose, we must live uncompromising lives and develop a deeply intimate relationship with God through Jesus Christ. We must fast, pray, and abandon our flesh (carnal-sin nature) and become more spiritually mature. Only then will we release God to destroy everything in us that blocks His will and purpose from being manifested in our lives. We sometimes make this journey more complicated than it really is. As my mother used to say, we just need to take it one day at a time, with the Lord as master. This is truly the call of a purposed woman.

Purposeful Thoughts

Remember to seek God in all things and ask Him for wisdom. Have the faith and confidence that if you ask for it, He will freely give it. James 1:5 states, "If any of you lack wisdom, let him ask of God, that giveth to all men liberally, and upbraideth not; and it shall be given him" (KJV). God doesn't want us to fall or stumble. It is His desire that we succeed and walk fully in the purposes He has for our lives. We all need God's wisdom to make the right decisions and choices in our lives. God instructs us not to lean to our own understanding about things but rather to acknowledge Him, and He will direct our paths. As women of wisdom, it is imperative that we don't depend on ourselves and our limited understanding and knowledge. Instead, we should lean on the wisdom that comes from God through the Holy Spirit, who leads us into all truth. What decisions or choices are you facing that require God's wisdom? Write them down and pray for wisdom. Believe that God will lead and guide you into His truth and success.

Devotional Notes

Questions

In what ways can you operate as the woman described in Proverbs 31, in your marriage, family, marketplace, community, or ministry?

Unfortunately, in our Western culture, we don't teach the importance of a name. Many of us fail to see the importance in naming and informing our children why they have their names, what their names mean, and our expectation that their lives will reflect the purpose of those names. This is true even among the spiritual, when we continue many of the same habits we had before Christ. Many of us have neither studied nor embraced the full understanding of how and why we were created by God. When we uncover these deep truths, we see God's wonderful creativity and omnipotence in shaping us for our purpose. As purposed women, we must grasp the life-changing truths revealed in the Word of God concerning our names, design, and purpose, as we walk in authority and power as the ambassadors of Christ and godly examples we were made to be. As a result of this purposeful and victorious living, our lives will exalt Christ and cause others to be transformed and experience new life in Him.

Questions

How can you walk in your "design" in your everyday life?

Home and family:

Marketplace:

Community:

Hope D. Blackwell

Purposeful Points from Chapter 1

1) I will exercise my supportive and life-giving qualities in the lives of those I influence in every arena of life. I will crucify my flesh, which will enable me to walk in the full potential of God's destiny for me as one who releases life, hope, and Christ to others.
2) Like the rib, I was designed to protect and assist. I will remember that a bruised or damaged rib will bring death to what it was designed to protect. My healing is critical. I will continually release all hurts, disappointments, and offenses. I choose to forgive, love, and be made whole. I will aid others without causing damage.
3) No matter how negative the situation or the person, I am called to rise above the situation and convey the character of Christ. This is not done by a simple "God bless you," "I'm blessed," or a mere hug. This supernatural ability is birthed out of an authentic love relationship and communication with the Holy Spirit, where the aim is to please God and genuinely love others as He loves us. He'll reveal what to say or do, when to say or do it, and how to say or do it. This requires a greater level of maturity in my walk with God. I welcome it!
4) Whatever or whoever I become intimate with will influence my identity and produce similar seeds. I will break negative and destructive ties in my life, and I will associate and bond with the things and people that promote spiritual health and growth.
5) My destiny and purpose is preordained by God. I will seek Him to identify and understand His plan for my life, and I will walk in obedience to His every directive.
6) When the fires of adversity come, I won't be discouraged; I will resolve that God's purpose is to burn off all flesh and destroy every hindrance that blocks His purpose for my life.

> I will praise You, for I am fearfully and wonderfully made; marvelous are Your works, and that my soul knows very well. (Psalms 139:14 KJV)

Chapter 2

The Thief of Purpose

Now the serpent was more subtle than any beast of the field which the Lord God had made. And he said unto the woman, "Hath God said ye shall not eat of every tree of the garden?" And the woman said unto the serpent, "We may eat of the fruit of the trees of the garden but of the fruit of the tree in the midst of the garden God hath said, Ye shall not eat of it, neither shall you touch it lest you surely die." The serpent said unto the woman, "Ye shall not surely die. For God knows that in the day ye eat thereof then your eyes shall be opened and ye shall be as Gods knowing good from evil." And when the woman saw the tree was good for food and it was pleasant to the eyes, and a tree desired to make one wise, she took of the fruit thereof and did eat and gave also unto her husband with her and he did eat. (Genesis 3:1-6 KJV)

In this chapter, we will examine the ultimate "thief of purpose," who was exposed in the Garden of Eden, and the violent crime that occurred there. We will analyze the effect this had on the purposes of Adam, Eve, and all mankind. In our study, we will reveal the four components of this crime that led to the fall of man and lead to many of our falls today.

They are:

1) Doubt
2) Deception

3) Diversion
4) Defeat

If we thoroughly reexamine some of the poor choices, unwise decisions, and impulsive actions we have taken, we will find that, in most instances, these four elements played a major role. We must understand that our choices, decisions, and actions lead us to either victory or defeat. Too often, we are blinded by our emotions, needs, and desires; they often cause us to make poor or impulsive decisions without taking time to fast, pray, or receive what God is saying through the Word, the Holy Spirit, or even our situation or circumstances. When we submit to our desires and our own will, not only do we hinder God's will, we impede someone else's path to purpose. Many times we fail to consider the possible long-term effects our decisions have on our destiny, as well as that of those around us. In this study, we will unveil some of the tricks the enemy uses in his attempt to obstruct the path to God's purpose in our lives and the lives of those to whom we are connected. We will expose this "thief of purpose" and discover how feeble and defeated he really is. As a result, we will become victorious in more of life's situations.

Doubt

Let's examine the first component: doubt. In Genesis 3, the first thing the serpent did was question Eve about God's instructions, getting her to doubt, which means to question or disbelieve.

This was his attempt to communicate with Eve (dialogue), to build a rapport with her. Genesis 3:1 reveals that the serpent was more subtle than any beast of the field that God had made. *Merriam-Webster's* defines *subtle* as "cunningly made or contrived, the opposite of innocent, or operating insidiously (awaiting a chance to entrap)." That is not quite like the snake many of us remember from our children's bedtime Bible stories, which depicted a silly-looking giant snake dangling from a tree and having a chat with Eve. In his original state, he probably stood upright, since one of God's curses was that he would roam around on his belly for the duration of his existence. It was that curse, found in Genesis 3:14, that led us to giving the devil the appearance of a snake. I imagine that he was an attractive, intriguing creature that could speak.

The serpent realized that he could win Eve over by paying attention and talking to her. This was his opportunity of a lifetime, to use dialogue to increase her doubt.

We must remain aware that the enemy is observing us and preparing the stage for our defeat. The serpent knew Eve was no dummy. He knew he had to be subtle and crafty to win her over. What better way to appeal to her than through her perceived needs. This is an example of detection, when the enemy finds a way to converse with us. Based on my spiritual imagination and evidence in the Word of God, it seems to me that the enemy detected that Eve and Adam communicated poorly. The serpent apparently satisfied a desire or a need within Eve because she undoubtedly talked to him. This dangerous and deadly conversation opened the door to doubt, which led to even greater desires of the flesh being awakened.

We must spend the time to communicate with and worship God so that the enemy has no room to play subtle tricks and work against us. We often make poor choices simply because we do not have two-way communication with God. We do all of the talking and fail to take the time to hear what He is saying. If we do hear Him, we often allow our will to overpower His. We miss the blessing of true intimacy with God. We let our needs, desires, and thoughts open the door to the enemy, who can then infuse our mind with doubt about the truth of God's Word and His promises for us. Doubt derails us from destiny and leads us to seek things that cause us to deviate from our original belief or plan.

Let's further explore this crime in the garden. Many women today do exactly what Eve did. Not only did she answer the serpent's question (which could have been a simple "yes" or "no"), she repeated the exact instructions God had given her, giving details of her conversation with God. But she also had the audacity to add something that God did *not* say to her. Eve revealed information to the serpent that opened the door and allowed him to attack her. This same error was made by Joseph, who shared his dreams and vision with his brothers (Genesis 37). Out of jealousy, they attempted to take his life by throwing him into a pit. Although God had a purpose for Joseph, who eventually prevailed, sharing that dream caused him to go through a difficult season. One of the enemy's tricks is to get you to bare all, to expose and uncover everything to the wrong people or at the wrong time. The more information you share, the more opportunity there is for Satan to probe into your emotions, desires, and carnal nature, and appeal to them in his attempts to derail you from a life of purpose. Remember, sharing the things of God with the wrong people at the wrong time is often costly. It can take you off the path to purpose or make it a lot rougher than God intended it to be.

Each time we enter into improper conversations or relationships, or begin to rely on our carnal-sin nature, doubt is the result:

- First, we question (or allow someone else to question) what we know to be the truth about God.
- We begin to dialogue with and listen to the lies of the enemy.
- The enemy then challenges the word of God and appeals to our flesh (unsurrendered emotions, ungodly desires, and carnal nature).
- Our flesh is aroused, and we began to disbelieve or ignore the truth of God's Word and His instructions to us.
- We discount the validity of God's Word and begin looking through eyes filled with lust, pride, and desire, leading to poor choices and decision making.

Purposeful Thoughts

How easily we slip into the cycle that leads to defeat! Can you think of a time in your life (past or present) when you have seen this pattern that leads to doubt? What about the times you were certain of God's instructions to you but somehow were derailed from His purpose and path? Could you identify with any of Eve's experiences in the garden? Make a commitment to walk away from the calamity of Eve and into the liberty available through new life in Jesus Christ.

Devotional Notes

Questions

1) How can you keep doubt from entering your mind?

2) What are some of God's instructions that will help you fight against doubt?

In the series of events that led to the crime in the garden, the seed of doubt was the beginning of Adam and Eve's defeat. Woman of God, it is no different today; doubt is at the root of most calamities. The Bible declares that "he who doubts is like a wave of the sea driven and tossed by the wind and let not that man suppose that he will receive anything from the Lord; he is a double-minded man, unstable in all his ways" (James 1:6-8 NKJV). When we doubt God's Word, we are actually saying that we don't believe in Him, that we are not willing to exercise faith, or that we choose to do our own thing. This, that is, choosing our desires and needs rather than His will in our lives, is what causes us to be tossed to and fro. Women of God, we must guard our minds and hearts against doubt. We should be mindful and discerning about what we share with others, particularly when God has given us specific directives concerning an issue. As stated previously, the enemy has no power over God's purpose for our lives, although, he does roam around looking for an opportunity to hijack our purpose. We must build ourselves up through prayers of faith, studying God's Word, and maintaining a godly lifestyle. As we strengthen our spirits, we will be equipped to overcome our fleshly desires when the enemy attempts to attack us.

Let's examine the second and third components, deception and diversion.

Deception and Diversion

In Genesis 3:1-4, notice how the serpent:

1) questions God's instructions;
2) listens to Eve repeat God's instructions;
3) disputes what God has told Eve, stating that it is false.

In Genesis 2:17, God told Adam, "but of the tree of the knowledge of good and evil you shall not eat, for in the day that you eat of it you shall surely die" (NKJV). Satan told her the opposite, saying "you will not surely die." As previously stated, this caused Eve to doubt the validity of God's word. Once she entered into a verbal exchange with the serpent, he deceived her and diverted her attention from God's instructions by making an appeal to her flesh (carnal-sin nature). More specifically, the appeal was to Eve's desire to have something she thought she was being deprived of (the fruit) and to attain something that she thought she should have (knowledge like God's), which was the very thing she already had access to. We must expose the root of this deception and how it occurred. *Merriam-Webster's* defines deception as "the act of deceiving." Deceive is defined by Merriam Webster as "to ensnare, or to cause to accept as true or valid what is false or invalid." *The Students' Hebrew and Chaldee Dictionary to the Old Testament* defines deceit as follows: "to lead astray, i.e., (mentally) to delude, or (morally) to seduce, beguile, greatly fill with wonder, or utterly amuse." *Vine's Expository Dictionary of Old and New Testament Words* (Reference Library edition) states, "Lusts are excited by deceit and although the lusts aren't deceitful in themselves, deceit is the source of their strength."

Genesis 3:5-6 reads, "For God knows that when you eat of it your eyes will be opened and you will be like God knowing good and evil. When the woman saw that the fruit of the tree was good for food and pleasing to the eye, and also desirable for gaining wisdom, she took some and ate" (NIV). Interestingly enough, verse 5 was not a lie told by the enemy, but the truth. Satan followed the lie that eating of the tree was not harmful with the truth about what the tree would do for Adam and Eve. We have to be cautious, because there is often some truth mixed in the enemy's suggestions. Consequently, in verse 6, Eve rationalized what she did; her judgment had become distorted. All Eve needed had already been provided in the garden by God; moreover, she had Him and was created in His image and likeness. However, her talk with the serpent led her to doubt God and believe that she would not surely die and would be like God, knowing good and evil, as if she needed to. I often wonder, since she already knew the good things about God and walked with Him daily, why did she desire to know the evil as well.

Women of God, we must be sensitive in those times that we desire to know both "good and evil." Perhaps God is trying to protect you from evil. Because Eve's desire to know good and evil was aroused, we now have to pray, as Jesus taught, "deliver us from evil." The thought of the ability to know all appealed to Eve, causing her to desire God's power. Eve was so convinced by the serpent that she disregarded God's promise that eating the fruit would lead to death. This crime in the garden is the first clear illustration of the lust of the flesh, the lust of the eyes, and the pride of life.

It is vital that we understand the war that rages between the flesh (our carnal-sin nature) and the spirit (our longing for the things of God). If we are not continually focused on God and led by the Holy Spirit, the flesh will win over the spirit every time. Romans 8:13 reads, "If you live according to the sinful nature you will die, but if you live according to the Spirit you will put to death the deeds of the body and you will live" (NIV). Romans 13:14 states, "but put on the Lord Jesus Christ, and make no provision for the flesh, to fulfill its lusts" (KJV). We must change our garments, put on Christ, and put away the deeds of our flesh or carnal-sin nature.

Genesis 3:6 reads, "When the woman saw the tree was good for food, and pleasing to the eye, and also desirable for gaining wisdom..." In this verse, let us examine the four main areas of Eve's vulnerability, which also plague us once we enter into the snares of the enemy and the trappings of our flesh:

1) Eve's reliance on natural sight as opposed to spiritual insight (the realization that the tree was good) speaks to her inability to see in the Spirit. After doubt and deception set in, Eve no longer avoided the tree as she had previously. Becoming separated from God and operating in her carnality caused her to have a distorted

view of God and the tree. She now saw the tree as something to attain, something good and desirable. When she lost sight, she lost vision.

2) The belief that the tree was good for food speaks to a woman's natural need for security and fulfillment, the desire to know all of our needs are met. This is a carnal desire that often undermines our faith. When deception set in, Eve's security in God became inadequate and she gained a desire for more. She saw the tree as another resource for her and Adam that would bring the security she now felt they needed. A relentless pursuit for natural security can often lead to the forfeiting of spiritual security, going against the spiritual law of Matthew 6:33, which instructs us to seek first the kingdom of God and its righteousness; then all other things will come to us.

3) Eve's lusts reveal her natural satisfaction and desire based on what she saw and now craved. *Merriam-Webster's* defines *desire* as "a conscious impulse toward something that promises enjoyment or satisfaction in its attainment." This was a deadly pleasure, aroused by the suggestions of the enemy and produced from the flesh. Desires themselves are not sinful, but those tainted by lust can become deadly.

4) Eve pursued wisdom and power, although she was designed by God and filled with His wisdom. She was made in His image and likeness and equipped with all that she needed. However, she was deceived into believing that she could be even wiser, knowing good and evil as God did. All that Adam and Eve knew was good. It's hard to imagine why Eve would have wanted to know the evil as well. Perhaps it was that evil, in and of itself, that aroused her curiosity with her knowledge; however, the attainment was not worth the loss. Seek to know the good things of God, and ask Him to deliver you from evil.

These accounts are thought-provoking and riveting, and too often are the basis for how we process things and make decisions, especially when separated from God and governed by our flesh and its deadly appetite. We must crucify our flesh in every situation or circumstance so that we don't fall into the deadly discussions that the enemy uses to appeal to our fleshly appetite. I love Paul's instructions in Colossians

3:5: "Therefore put to death your members which are on the earth: fornication, uncleanness, passion, evil desire, and covetousness, which is idolatry. Because of these things the wrath of God is coming upon the sons of disobedience, in which you yourselves once walked when you lived in them." We must remember these "members" are always at war within us, and we must take the responsibility of subjecting them to the Holy Spirit and the word of God, so that we will be victorious over the enemy and the flesh! It is our responsibility to walk in an understanding, reverent, and righteous lifestyle in Christ Jesus.

Questions

1) How can you avoid being deceived and diverted from God's purpose of God for your life?

2) Refer to the Scripture and identify areas where the enemy has attempted to deceive you or has been successful at deceiving you? Then release these areas to God, and ask him to free you from shame and guilt, and give you the strength to address the consequences and walk in victory.

Purposeful Thoughts

It's easy to go off course when we have unsurrendered emotions that cause us to walk in our carnal nature. This is the road that leads us to the works of the flesh (adultery, fornication, uncleanness, lasciviousness, idolatry, witchcraft, hatred, variance, emulations, wrath, strife, seditions, heresies, envy, murders, drunkenness, revelry, etc., described in Galatians 5:19-21). The Bible instructs us that those who practice these things will not inherit the kingdom of God. Since Christ suffered for us in the flesh, we should arm ourselves with the same mind (1 Peter 4:1-2), and no longer live the rest of our time lusting for the things of men, but seeking the will of God. Be mindful that this is bigger than your purpose on earth; it also refers to the quality of your eternity. A wonderful and glorious characteristic of our God is His mercy. He states in Romans 8:1: "There is therefore now no condemnation to those who are in Christ Jesus, who walk not according to the flesh but according to the Spirit" (MKJV). So you can be free from the lusts and works of the flesh and walk in victory over sin, relying on the power of God through the Holy Spirit. Let us walk in Galatians 5:1, which states, "stand fast therefore in the liberty with which Christ has made us free, and do not again be held with the yoke of bondage" (MKJV). Once in liberty, fulfill the scripture, which advises against using your freedom for an occasion of the flesh. What are some areas of the flesh that need surrendering in your life?

Devotional Notes

Giving in to ungodly desires and the lusts of our flesh fuels the passions of our sinful nature. The more we yield to them, the more other areas of carnality are awakened within us. This is why we must be careful to judge all things by the Spirit. Our desires will change when we put God first in everything and spend time with Him. Imagine how it could have been if Eve had remained in the garden, worshipping and communing with God daily. Psalms 37:4 reads, "Delight yourself in the Lord and He will give you the desires of your heart" (KJV). When you delight yourself in the Lord, your desires become centered on Him; they become the same as His. So in actuality your heart is changed. Your desires are no longer the foolish things of the flesh (carnal-sin nature) or things that have no real meaning or significance. Paul teaches us that if the Spirit of God lives in us, we will not be controlled by sinful nature, but by the Spirit; and if Christ lives within us, our flesh is dead, yet our spirit is alive (Romans 8:9-11 KJV).

Let us examine the last component of the crime in the garden and the one with the greatest impact:

Defeat

Note the following D's that led to the final D of defeat in the crime in the garden:

1) Detection: The enemy perceived a weakness in Eve.
2) Dialogue: Eve communicated with the enemy.
3) Doubt: She considered the enemy's suggestions, which caused her to disregard the instructions of God and validity of His word.
4) Deception: She was enticed into accepting a lie as the truth by the crafty and subtle connotations of the enemy.
5) Desire: Her carnal human nature was aroused.
6) Discontentment: She felt dissatisfied with what God had given her, and her dissatisfaction caused her to crave something more.
7) Disobedience: She acted in opposition to God's instructions.
8) Diversion: She was taken off the course that God had set for her and Adam.
9) Death: Her decisions led to spiritual death and separation from God.
10) Disguise: The shame of their sin caused Adam and Eve to cover themselves and hide from God.

Defeat is inevitable once we have allowed the previous D's to operate in our lives. The enemy wants to see us suffer defeat, so that we will fail to walk in the purposes and plans God has ordained for His children. Satan knows that if we allow ourselves to be open to his enticements that our demise will soon follow. His goal is to cause our separation from God, which is often followed by shame and guilt, distancing us even further.

Genesis 2:17 records the following words of God: "you must not eat of the tree of the knowledge of good and evil, for when you eat of it you will surely die" (NIV). We know that God spared Adam and Eve from physical death. However, they were defeated by the enemy because they allowed themselves to be deceived and led astray by Satan's enticements, which caused their separation from God. Satan was more interested in their spiritual demise and separation from God than in their physical death. The enemy is relentless in his attempts to separate us from God through sin and its entrapments; he knows that guilt, shame, and separation will follow and divert us from our kingdom purpose.

As women of purpose, we must know the areas and periods of vulnerability in our lives. Examples include seasons of grief, loss, loneliness, illness, or when we are emotionally challenged by situations or circumstances. While we know that we are victorious through Christ Jesus, we must remain aware of the warnings in 1 Peter 5:8: that we are to be sober and watchful because our adversary, who is the devil, is prowling around like a roaring lion, seeking someone to devour. Friend, we are not exempt from his attempts, but rather are his targets. In times of weariness, trials, and temptation, we must make the spiritual preparations described in Ephesians 6:10-20 that will cause us to stand victorious against the enemy in his appeal:

> Finally, my brethren, be strong in the Lord, and in the power of his might. Put on the whole armour of God, that ye may be able to stand against the wiles of the devil. For we wrestle not against flesh and blood, but against principalities, against powers, against the rulers of the darkness of this world, against spiritual wickedness in high places. Wherefore take unto you the whole armour of God, that ye may be able to withstand in the evil day, and having done all, to stand. Stand therefore, having your loins girt about with truth, and having on the breastplate of righteousness; And your feet shod with the preparation of the gospel of peace; Above all, taking the shield of faith, wherewith ye shall be able to quench all the fiery darts of the wicked. And take the helmet of salvation, and the sword of the Spirit, which is the word of God: Praying always with all prayer and supplication in the Spirit, and watching thereunto with all perseverance and supplication for all saints; And for me, that utterance may be given unto me, that I may open my mouth boldly, to make known the mystery of the gospel, For which I am an ambassador in bonds: that therein I may speak boldly, as I ought to speak. (KJV)

Consider this interesting but common scenario: You are a single woman of God, who is not dating. You are aware of what the Word of God says about relationships, fornication, and your body. You also understand what it takes to be in an equally yoked (spiritually compatible) relationship. You meet a handsome, single, and saved (or even unsaved) man. You begin to converse with him, revealing too much information about yourself. You reveal your vision, weaknesses, heartaches, accomplishments, strengths, etc. The conversations quickly lead to dating, which in turn, leads to the arousal of unawakened sensual desires.

Unfortunately, at this stage, many Christian women engage in sexual encounters and even go as far as to move in with their "friends." That is a fast track to defeat and the death of purpose. Like Eve, you become consumed with satisfying your own perceived needs and desires, which are now tainted. Your unstable emotions and ungodly desires are exposed, and your innermost yearnings are now the motivation for your decision-making. Despite how unequally yoked you may be, like Eve, you disregard the validity of God's word, and rationalize the relationship, continuing in disobedience.

This is why God instructs us not to awaken love before it is time (Song of Solomon 8:4 KJV). Women who remain devoted to God and are led by Him avoid resorting to such behavior. They make the choice to exercise discipline, relying on the keeping power of the Holy Spirit coupled with wise decision making, which protect them from the premature awakening of emotions and feelings and block certain desires from being aroused. During that time of waiting, these desires are in what I call the "sleep mode." The desire to please and honor God motivates their discipline. Walking in the Spirit keeps them from fulfilling the desires of the flesh. No one is saying by any means that this process is easy, only that it is possible.

In this type of scenario the following is probably true about the relationship:

1) You did not earnestly pray about the person, or you prayed seeking affirmation, not confirmation or instruction.
2) You were not at the level of wholeness and intimacy with God that is required before entertaining a relationship.

3) There was evidence early on that this person was not God's choice for you.
4) You were giving more to that relationship than you were giving to God.

Any of these conditions compromise God's anointing of you and His purpose for your life, making it easy for the enemy to divert you from your set course. Under these conditions, you are blind to the enemy's involvement in the situation because you are focused primarily on yourself and your "friend" (although he really isn't acting as a true friend at all). Regretfully, in my many encounters with Christian women of varied social status, I have found countless to be so deficient in the area of true intimacy with God that it is easy for men to effortlessly divert them from a path of righteousness, and many do. I would be remiss in my assignment if I did not tell you that in our society, women desiring other women has become increasingly prevalent as well. Don't be deceived, the penalty for the crime and the course of defeat is the same, whether the desire is for a man or a woman.

In any case, in our scenario, you go on to entertain your friend's questions and suggestions, which further incite compromise and doubt. The suggestions come in the form of a deceptive rationale such as, "God knows our hearts"; "we really love each other and are planning to get married anyway"; and "I'm only going to be with him once", or the famous "I know he is my husband", often used by women who believe God has revealed whom their husband is, as if that justifies the compromise. The most ridiculous rationale, which was once seemingly exclusive to men, but is increasingly the mindset of women as well, is: "I have needs. God gave us these desires; they're natural." Granted the needs are natural—naturally carnal and sinful when not controlled and disciplined by the Holy Spirit and in alignment with the Word of God.

We must get to the place where we are not so easily defeated by others, the devil, or even ourselves. Remember, according to the Word of God, we have three enemies: the world, the flesh (carnal-sin nature), and Satan. In most cases, Satan has no need to engage us because we are already being attacked and defeated by our flesh. It is vital for us to strengthen our spirits by staying focused on the things of God. We often fuel up the soul tank with things that appease our flesh instead of the filling up our spirit tank, which will produce life and peace. Ask yourself: *What am I reading? What am I listening to? What am I watching? What am I meditating on? Do these things strengthen the flesh or the spirit?* How you answer those questions will reveal whether you will walk in the joy of victory or the sad agony of defeat! I am reminded of a poem by an unknown US marine that states, "Two natures beat within my chest, one is cursed, one is blessed; one I love, the other I hate, but the one I feed will dominate."

Purposeful Thoughts

Allow your spirit to win the battle against your flesh. What you feed grows, and what you starve dies. Whichever one you strengthen will win. In your devotional notes take into consideration the questions for reflection in the previous paragraph, and make note of the things that need to be starved or fed in your life. Then take one day at a time, and just do it. The Word of God declares you can do all things through Christ, who strengthens you.

Questions

1) Reflect on defeat you've experienced in the past situations. Were any of the Ds present in your situation? If so, which ones? How did you overcome them?

2) What can you do in the future to avoid the traps set by the enemy that could cause your demise?

It is so important to accept the reality that sometimes we "miss the mark" in life. Often, we operate out of desire and may fail to analyze situations wisely. However, we are given opportunities to repent, be restored, and refocus on God's plans for us. Because of God's mercy, we often are saved from many consequences of our actions as well as the adverse effects of being used and abused by others. *Merriam Webster's* defines *mercy* as compassion or forbearance shown especially to an offender or to one subject to one's power; *also*: lenient or compassionate. God's mercy is always evident in our lives. He steps between us and the penalty for our actions, preventing us from feeling the full effects or consequences. We must remember that when we fall down it is because of God's grace that we can get back up and continue to move forward. Grace, in all of its beauty, is defined by *Merriam Webster's* as "unmerited divine assistance given to humans for their regeneration or sanctification."

Let us look at how Paul shares the beauty of God's grace and mercy to the believers in Rome in Romans 5:1-21:

> Therefore, since we have been made righteous through his faithfulness combined with our faith, we have peace with God through our Lord Jesus Christ. We have access by faith into this grace in which we stand through him, and we boast in the hope of God's glory. But not only that! We even take pride in our problems, because we know that trouble produces endurance, endurance produces character, and character produces hope. This hope doesn't put us to shame, because the love of God has been poured out in our hearts through the Holy Spirit, who has been given to us. While we were still weak, at the right moment, Christ died for ungodly people. It isn't often that someone will die for a righteous person, though maybe someone might dare to die for a good person. But God shows his love for us, because while we were still sinners Christ died for us. So, now that we have been made righteous by his blood, we can be even more certain that we will be saved from God's wrath through him. If we were reconciled to God through the death of his Son while we were still enemies, now that we have been reconciled, how much more certain is it that we will be saved by his life? And not only that: we even take pride in God through our Lord Jesus Christ, the one through whom we now have

a restored relationship with God. So, in the same way that sin entered the world through one person, and death came through sin, so death spread to all human beings with the result that all sinned. Although sin was in the world, since there was no Law, it wasn't taken into account until the Law came. But death ruled from Adam until Moses, even over those who didn't sin in the same way Adam did—Adam was a type of the one who was coming. But the free gift of Christ isn't like Adam's failure. If many people died through what one person did wrong, God's grace is multiplied even more for many people with the gift—of the one person Jesus Christ—that comes through grace. The gift isn't like the consequences of one person's sin. The judgment that came from one person's sin led to punishment, but the free gift that came out of many failures led to the verdict of acquittal. If death ruled because of one person's failure, those who receive the multiplied grace and the gift of righteousness will even more certainly rule in life through the one person Jesus Christ. So now the righteous requirements necessary for life are met for everyone through the righteous act of one person, just as judgment fell on everyone through the failure of one person. Many people were made righteous through the obedience of one person, just as many people were made sinners through the disobedience of one person. The Law stepped in to amplify the failure, but where sin increased, grace multiplied even more. The result is that grace will rule through God's righteousness, leading to eternal life through Jesus Christ our Lord, just as sin ruled in death. (CEB)

Woman of God, remember God's word in Luke 10:19: "Behold, I give unto you power to tread on serpents and scorpions, and over all the power of the enemy: and nothing shall by any means hurt you" (KJV). First be sure to get wisdom, as the Bible teaches us, and then exercise your authority over Satan's demonic strategies and influences. Finally, receive the mercy of God and the gift of Jesus Christ (the anointed one), and walk in the freedom and grace that God releases to those who accept His son Jesus, the gift of righteousness, through which all must come to know Him.

Purposeful Points from Chapter 2

1) I will not allow myself to share deep intimate thoughts hastily. I understand that if I don't use caution, I could share the wrong things with the wrong people at the wrong time, causing diversion. I will follow the instructions in Proverbs 4:23 to guard my heart diligently, knowing that out of it flows the issues of life.
2) I will obey the instructions of God. I will not allow any person, situation, or circumstance to cause me to question God's Word, instructions, or will for my life.
3) I will not allow the desires of my flesh (carnal-sin nature) to alter my decisions or the choices I make. I will spend time in prayer and develop a more intimate relationship with God so that I will know His voice and be led by His Spirit.
4) I will continually nurture my spirit in the things of God, meditate on His Word, and listen to hymns, worship songs, and other spiritual messages and teachings. I will not read, watch, or digest things that feed the flesh and its sensual desires. I make a commitment to starve the flesh and feed the spirit, understanding that the stronger of the two will always win.
5) I will recognize and rebuke the enemy when he comes. I will spiritually mature so regardless of how subtle or appealing the enemy presents himself, I can discern with accuracy what is really happening, continue in godliness, and walk in the victory.
6) I will set high standards for myself and will not deviate from them. I will exercise discipline. I will not give in or give up. I will learn the Word of God and what He desires "for me" and also "me for." I will not settle for anything less than God's perfect will for my life.

> Delight yourself also in the Lord, and He shall give you the desires of your heart. (Psalms 37:4 NKJV)

Chapter 3

The Consequences of Misdirected Emotions

. . . She took of the fruit thereof and did eat, and gave also unto her husband with her and he did eat. And the eyes of them were opened and they knew that they were naked; and they sewed fig leaves together and made themselves aprons. And they heard the voice of the Lord God walking in the garden in the cool of the day: and Adam and his wife hid themselves from the presence of the Lord God amongst the trees of the garden. (Genesis 3:6-8 KJV)

Unto the woman he said, "I will greatly multiply thy sorrow and thy conception; in sorrow thou shalt bring forth children; and thy desire shall be to thy husband and he shall rule over you." (Genesis 3:16 KJV)

Therefore the Lord God sent him forth from the garden of Eden, to till the ground from whence he was taken. So he drove out the man; and he placed at the east of the garden of Eden Cherubims and a flaming sword which turned every way to keep the way of the tree of life. (Genesis 3:23, 24 KJV)

There are consequences to every act of disobedience. We have suffered consequences for disobeying since childhood and throughout our adult lives, including our lives as maturing Christians. As discussed in chapter 2, when we are led astray by our emotions, desires, and the lusts of our flesh, disobedience is inevitable. Although the reality of our emotions exists, and we need not pretend they don't, we must channel them toward God in order to develop the heart and mind of Christ. We have to curse the "follow your heart" mentality. Jeremiah 17:9 reads, "The heart is deceitful above all things and beyond cure, who can understand it?" (NIV). The latter portion of the same verse in the King James Version asks, "who can trust in it?" The book of Psalms records David's pleas to God for a new heart. In Psalms 86:11, he requests "an undivided heart"; in Psalms 51:10, "a pure heart"; and in Psalms 51:17, "a broken and contrite heart" (NIV).

In the book of Ezekiel, God declared that after He had cleansed and purified the people of Israel, He would give them a new heart and Spirit. We must submit our hearts to God for purification and cleansing. Instead of following our hearts, we should follow God's commands and the lead of the Holy Spirit. The Bible states that the heart is the innermost seat of our emotions and desires. When unsurrendered to God and His word, our emotions and desires become misdirected and a danger to our fulfillment of purpose, often producing sin. We know from Romans 6:23 that the consequence of sin is death. First Peter 2:11 urges us to abstain from sinful desires because they war against the things of the Spirit.

I've often wondered if Eve had been in closer communion and communication with God, would she have been more protective of God's purposes for her and Adam and less susceptible to the serpent's ploys. Perhaps she would have been unshakeable in her resolve concerning God's instructions and less likely to fall for the beguiling serpent. Unfortunately for us all, once she was deceived and led astray by her desires, there was havoc in the garden and in the progression of all mankind. It is vital that we explore the consequences of her yielding to the desires of her flesh. Many of us are still suffering from those same consequences.

As previously discussed, after being deceived in her thinking, Eve believed the tree to be a benefit rather than the detriment God said it would be. So with tainted understanding, she immediately sought to share this wonderfully, beneficial fruit with her husband. I do not believe that Eve intentionally desired, in any way, to destroy Adam or their fate. Consider what we learned in chapter 1. Eve was created to be Adam's helper and protector and a giver of life. She was made by the hand and wisdom of God to compliment Adam. Reflect on what we learned in the previous chapter about the broken or damaged rib, which can actually destroy what it is designed to protect. Eve was so deceived by the enemy and her own newly developed desires that she was attempting to help (at least she thought so). But her damaged state led to the destruction of the fulfillment of purpose for Adam, the one she was created to help and protect. Inevitably, this led to her destruction as well. She never considered the consequences of her actions, because she was operating in her carnal nature, or what I call "misdirected emotions."

Women of God, I am not saying that Eve was solely responsible for the crime that caused the fall of man. There is an element that Adam was also guilty of perpetrating, but please understand actually neither of them is to be fully blamed. Read *Back to the Garden, the Man, the Purpose*, published 2004 by Hope D. Blackwell, to understand the role and responsibility of Adam in the garden. However, God clearly identifies the real culprit in the scripture in Genesis 3:14, when He looks at the serpent and says, "cursed are you because you did this"! However, in our vital role as helpers, we must accept responsibility when we allow ourselves to be led astray and robbed of purpose right before our eyes. Although the Word of God states that God works for the good of those who love Him and are called to His purpose, He never approves our surrendering to the enemy's attempts to rob us of purpose. Our submission to Satan's tactics occurs when we are not fasting, praying, studying the Word of God, and walking in obedience. We must remember the enemy looks for a crack or place in which to squeeze; therefore we are to guard our hearts and minds at all times. Remember, even Jesus fasted to prepare himself for purpose and the attacks of Satan, who came to tempt him during his forty days of fasting in the wilderness. Because of His preparation, Jesus was able to declare in John 14:30, "when the ruler of this world comes, he has nothing in me" (NKJV). Jesus left no space in His life or ministry for Satan to have a point of connection.

Questions

1) Identify some of the negative effects misdirected emotions can have in women and those that have caused you to fall and suffer serious consequences in your life.

2) What are things that you can do to ensure that you are operating in the Spirit and not in the flesh or emotions?

Purposeful Thoughts

Emotions are a vital part of life and were given to us by God. We were created in His image, and He has emotions. The Bible says in John 3:16: "For God so loved the world that He gave His only begotten son that whosoever believeth in him should not perish but have everlasting life" (KJV). His love for us, which is one of the greatest motivating emotions, caused Him to give us His everything. His emotion provoked an action. Like God, we should also use our emotions to connect what is spiritual to the natural, causing the manifestation of God's purpose and plans. When they are submitted to God, our emotions can help us fulfill His purposes, as Jesus Christ demonstrated on earth. We must surrender our emotions and allow the Holy Spirit to lead us to truth, wisdom, and balance. Emotions can be used for good when we seek God for His desires, as opposed to ours. Too often, however, unsurrendered emotions paralyze our thought processes and make us spiritually weak. This is why we are instructed in 2 Corinthians 10:5 to bring every thought into the obedience of Jesus Christ. This verse further states that once our obedience has been fulfilled, there will be a readiness to revenge all disobedience. Woman of God, make the choice not to operate in mere feelings, but to seek God for spiritual leadership that will keep you free from emotionalism and poor decision making. As women, our emotions can be the very catalyst that leads to spiritual death. However, once they are made whole in Christ, they can help us release His love and life. In your devotional notes, consider things that need to be surrendered to God in this area. You are on the road to becoming a purposed woman!

Devotional Notes

After disobedience, which often follows emotionalism and poor choices, sin emerges, and innocence departs. Genesis 3:7 reads, "The eyes of both of them were opened and they knew that they were naked; and they sewed fig leaves together and made themselves aprons" (NIV). *Merriam-Webster's* defines *naked* as "devoid of covering or lacking confirmation or support." Adam and Eve knew they were naked and without covering. This passage of Scripture reveals that after we have engaged in sin and disobedience, we become mentally and spiritually aware that we have shifted from the safety and comfort of God, our covering.

When we overtly disobey God and do not repent, we forfeit His protection and open the door to repeated sin and its strongholds. We are not spared from the consequences of our actions or misdirected emotions. Consider the number of issues in our lives that are consequences of our disobedience; not circumstances prompted by God, the devil, our enemies, or the world, but simply the results of choices and decisions that we made based on ignorance and misdirected emotions. Many things are affected by sin but can be avoided if we walk away victoriously in obedience to God's commands and stay under His covering. Our failure to do so can damage critical areas in our lives, such as marriage, family, relationships, parenting, health, finances, spiritual maturity, and countless others.

Just as Adam and Eve made natural coverings (with fig leaves) for themselves after they discovered they were naked, we too are often guilty of this same attempt to cover up when we have fallen into disobedience and sin. Many of us use the church as a "covering," or a cover-up, using participation in church activities, committees, and other rituals to mask our sin and disobedience. We are not ready to repent and obey, so we remain unrepentant, hiding among the trees as did Adam and Eve. Regrettably, as perpetrators of fraud, we give the false appearance that we are productive and in right standing with God. In actuality, however, we will not come clean with Him, due to the willful disobedience that has produced an inability to face Him. Like Adam and Eve, we avoid intimacy with God in the hope that He will overlook our sin, while we continue our actions without repenting, without turning away from the sin. These actions lead us further from God. The continuation of "church as usual" in the midst of sinful behavior leads to self-deceit, which can lead to pride and hypocritical living. We are unable to worship the Father in spirit and in truth and thus nullify any attempt at true worship. Genesis 3:8 states, "they hid themselves from the presence of the Lord God among the trees in the garden" (NKJV). This reveals some additional consequences of sin and disobedience: guilt, shame, fear, and separation. Sin causes us to feel naked and exposed in shame, resulting in a desire to hide. Because this desire is prompted by our flesh (carnal-sin nature), it instinctively opposes the desire to repent, which would lead to restoration, peace, and covering. This speaks to the D component, disguise, shared in chapter 2.

Having been created in the image of God, who is love, Adam and Eve were no doubt filled with love for God and the things of God. However, after their disobedience they became aware that their once perfect relationship with God no longer existed as they knew it. Their eyes had become opened to good and evil, just as God stated. The way they once viewed themselves had been tainted by intimacy with the serpent and disobedience. Separated by sin, they became aware of the absence of God's Spirit, which led to feelings of guilt, shame, and fear, causing them to attempt to hide from God. The desire to hide is evidence of sin's ability to keep us separated from God, which leads to spiritual death. Adam and Eve were so stained by sin they feared approaching God; they knew He was (and is) the Light that reveals all truth. Because darkness and light are opposed to one another, our communion with God is hindered when we are in darkness. Moreover, continuing in sin strains other relationships, limiting the possibility of purposeful living. Often we think when the Spirit of Truth exposes our sin, He will leave us embarrassed and disgraced. This is a lie and trick of the enemy and a result of not knowing or trusting God's promise in 1 John 1:9, which states that, "when we confess our sins, He is faithful and just to forgive us our sins and cleanse us from all unrighteousness."(NKJV) When we fall further in the pit of shame produced by sin, we lose the understanding of our wonderful Savior as well as His compassion, mercy, and redemptive power. Shame and conviction are naturally felt responses to sin; however guilt and condemnation are the enemy's attempt to keep us further separated from God.

I am reminded of the accounts of Moses and the children of Israel in Exodus 20 and 21. Even after having seen and known our great God intimately, because they knew they had not truly "washed their clothes" (prepared to meet Jehovah) and were still stained with the filth of Egypt (the old mentality of sin and idolatry), when the children of Israel heard the thunder and saw the lightning and the mountain smoking, "they removed, and stood afar off" (Exodus 20:18 KJV). They actually told Moses, "if you speak to us we will hear, but let not God speak to us or we will die" (Exodus 20:19 NASB). Even after Moses admonished them to fear not, the Scripture declares that when Moses approached, the people stood far away. Once again, we see an example of a people whose separation from God compelled them to hide rather than approach Him with humility, reverence, and repentance, which caused an even greater separation from God.

One of the awesome characteristics of our great God is His mercy, which is evident not only in the New Testament but throughout the Bible. We know that there were consequences to Adam and Eve's sin, but God still loved them and covered them, even after exposing their disobedience. There also is no doubt that God was angry with the children of Israel, but He still wanted them to draw near to Him. He wanted them to remain His people. He would be their God, and He could dwell among them, a kingdom of priests and a holy nation. He continually demonstrates His love for us in overwhelming ways. The Bible declares in Romans 5:8: "But God commendeth His love toward us, in that, while we were yet sinners, Christ died for us" (KJV). Our disobedience causes us to fear God (in the full definition of being afraid or scared); however, if we feared (i.e., holy fear meaning reverence)

God, we would have nothing to fear because we would be embraced by His mercy and love and empowered for purpose by His grace.

We must renounce the spirit of fear, and pick up holy fear, with understanding. Let us bring light to the darkness of sin by approaching the throne and repenting. It is then that we too can be covered by our great and merciful God. No longer allow yourself to be separated by hiding and missing your healing for fear of embracing our loving and merciful God.

Purposeful Thoughts

The Bible distinctly states in Genesis 2:25: "And they were both naked, the man and his wife, and not ashamed." Genesis 3:10 states, "And he said, I heard thy voice in the garden, and I was afraid, because I was naked; and I hid myself." Anyone walking with God in obedience to His commands and instructions has a childlike freedom. There is a level of purity and innocence that causes you to be naked (completely exposed) before God and man, unashamed. Consider babies who are free and without shame in the purity and innocence of their nakedness. However, if they are violated, abused, or deceived into releasing the treasure of that innocence, they feel a need to hide, retreat, and cover themselves in hopes that it will remove the feeling of shame. But they cannot dismiss it, which often leads to further violations.

Even as adults who have been set free from the sins of Adam and Eve through the blood of Christ, we can relate to children's experiences because they are often repeated in situations throughout our lives. Satan's scheme in the garden was to cause disobedience that would break the fellowship between God and man and bring death to the plans and purpose of God. When Adam and Eve hid from God, they fell deeper into Satan's scheme. Too often, after sin and disobedience, we become prey in the enemy's trap to keep us hiding and in a state of separation. His condemnation, coupled with our guilt, cause us to cover up or hide, which robs us of the healing, restoration, and covering of Jesus Christ. Be encouraged; no matter what you've done or how bad things seem, God wants you near Him. Nothing can separate you from the love of our most merciful God. The Bible declares in 1 John 1:9: "If we confess our sins, He is faithful and just to forgive us our sins, and to cleanse us from all unrighteousness" (KJV). I pray that you will genuinely repent of sin, come out of hiding, and receive the love and mercy of God. Throughout time, God has gone through great measures to show us the great love He has for us. Even when we sin, murmur, and complain, He never alters or changes His original plan for us, despite our foolishness. He is just waiting for us to "get it." The Bible declares in Isaiah 43:25: "I, even I, am He that blotteth out your transgressions for mine own sake, and I will not remember your sins" (KJV). Remember friend, God has plans and a purpose for your life, and for His own name's sake He wants to restore you so you can walk in those plans. Great is His mercy and grace toward us. Get naked before God, and let Him cover you!

Questions

1) What are some things that you do in your attempts to hide from God? What are some of the modern day "trees" that you have hidden under?

2) How can you come out of shame and be naked (i.e., completely open and exposed) before God, ensuring His forgiveness and protection? Will you?

We have examined some consequences of the sin that resulted from misdirected emotions and disobedience. Now let us further explore and understand how we, as women on a purposed journey, are affected by the consequences of God's judgment, which were a result of Eve's decisions.

Many physicians do a thorough job of explaining the many processes that are unique to women (i.e., hormones, conception, childbirth, mothering). However, the most accurate and true explanation is found in the scriptural accounts of the events that took place in the Garden of Eden. It is there that we will uncover the natural cause and effect of God's judgment imposed on Eve as well as its spiritual ramifications, which have had and shall continue to have an impact on every woman since Eve. As women pursuing purpose, we must fully understand these truths.

In Genesis 3:16, we find the pronouncement of God's judgment on Eve as a result of her sin. We will study the sentence imposed on Eve in two parts. This is the first part of her punishment, as declared by God: "I will greatly multiply thy sorrow and thy conception; in sorrow thou shalt bring forth children."

Women of God, for generations we have witnessed the manifestation of this declaration in both the natural and the spiritual. We can easily remember when we, or some other dear sister, was in the delivery room trying to endure the pain and discomfort of the birthing process, which Eve was responsible for! So let us begin by exploring the natural application of this passage in order to receive the spiritual revelation found within it.

In our examination of this Scripture, we find that pain and sorrow is promised throughout the entire child-birthing process. We have always considered this process as being from conception through birth; however, in actuality, it begins prior to the nine-month window. It starts at puberty when the female body undergoes a transformation, which enables the production of the egg necessary for conception. After the initiation of this process, it becomes a recurring cycle of preparation for conception. Many of us consider this a curse, and we do so because of the physical distress, hygiene concerns, emotional instability, and in some cases the downright painful process that our body endures to prepare itself for conception. Even in its beauty, many women experience the "sorrow," the Scripture promises. The truth to note is whether we ever conceive or not, we are still recipients of the judgment imposed on Eve.

The next progression in this process is the "sorrow" experienced during the preparation for birth that follows conception. The intimacy between a man and a woman progresses to a physical bonding that leads to conception. The intended and most God-honoring process for this exchange is the time spent together between a husband and wife, cultivating love, physical intimacy, and communication. This level of intimacy leads them to share their spirit, soul, and body, the two becoming one in every way; the latter progression being the process by which the seed of the man fertilizes the egg that is within the womb of the woman, and consequently life is conceived. After a period of growth and development, the body is ready to birth (deliver) new life. Throughout this stage, the body has been stretched, pulled, cramped, kicked, disfigured, and greatly inflated. As many of us can attest, this beautiful process is not always pleasant, with the most challenging days still ahead. Inevitably, the stage of delivery comes and this is the ultimate point of pain, resulting in temporary "sorrow," as God declared in the garden. Nevertheless, after a successful delivery, the blessing and treasure that was birthed during the pain is life, with the potential to transform, have an impact on, and affect the lives of countless others, bringing us to tears of joy after our tears of pain.

Let us consider the same process in the spiritual realm. God saves us, renews our spirit, and begins to realign our thinking about His truths. He created us with a purpose and will give us a *rhema* (specific) word. This can be referred to as a seed of promise. As stated in Luke 8:11, " . . . the seed is the word of God" (NIV).

As in childbirth, our spirit experiences changes that cause discomfort, challenges, pain, and occasionally sorrow as we prepare to receive the seed of promise. There are changes and preparation for this conception that are similar to those in the other. There is a level of intimacy that is necessary prior to conception. We must engage Christ intimately to ensure conception. This level of intimacy can only be achieved when we spend time with Him in praise, worship, prayer, and study. Only then will we be impregnated with His promise and purpose for our lives. Once you become a woman of God through salvation and receive the seed of promise, which is the word of God, you begin the process of transformation in which you will eventually give birth to your purpose and destiny in God. As in childbirth, this process can be difficult and challenging, stretching our faith, draining our emotions, and causing pain to our flesh. However, just as God declared in the garden about childbirth, so it is with the spiritual birth. This process is required to prepare us for our expected end. The seed of promise, placed within us during our time of relationship and intimacy with God, requires growth, development, and maturity. As in childbirth, at the appointed time, the birth (delivery) of purpose is inevitable. After a successful delivery, the blessings birthed out of the pain are larger than life, with the potential to change, impact, and affect the lives of countless others.

Women of God, we must consider the blessing on the other side of the mountain, the light at the end of the tunnel, the healing after the breaking. If Mary's alabaster box had never been broken, the sweet fragrance that anointed our Lord would never have been released to bless Him in such a way that touched His heart so deeply. Sometimes the box of our lives gets shattered, bringing us pain, but there are deep treasures beyond the exterior of our lives, circumstances, and situations that release the fragrance that glorifies our Lord. No one knows better than our God how to bring the treasures hidden within us to the surface. Like the blessings of children, the blessings of God's promise make the struggle and the pain more than worth it. Let God have His way, and go through the process of pain to purpose. After the breaking comes the blessing and birthing of something wonderful, filled with great purpose.

Purposeful Thoughts

The Bible declares in John 12:24, 25: "Verily, verily, I say unto you, except a corn of wheat fall into the ground and die, it abideth alone; but if it dies, it bringeth forth much fruit" (KJV). Figuratively speaking, we have to die in order to live. In order to walk in our purpose in Christ and bring forth fruit, everything about us must die. This includes but is not limited to our will, desires, emotions, ambitions, and anything we have not surrendered to Him. When you feel that you've been driven into the ground, covered up, and seem to be forgotten, remember that you have not been buried, but planted by the Father! You can count on the Son of God shining down upon you to nourish and prepare you to spring up right on schedule. It is God's will to resurrect us at the appropriate time. Think of the "dying" places in your life, and notate the stretching situations that you've experienced in preparation for God's purpose for your life to blossom. Be encouraged, His will is at work in your life even in circumstances that seem dead. Remember that the grain of wheat must first fall into the ground and die in order to produce. Woman of God, He is doing it for you in the dying place!

Questions

1) What are some ways that you sense God stretching you in preparation for His purposes for your life?

2) Consider the alabaster box, which was very beautiful, yet was broken to release the fragrance that was used to anoint the feet of Christ. What are some the things that you deemed to be "the box" in your life that now must be broken to release the very thing that will bless you and advance God's purposes for your life?

Let us examine another consequence that we must understand clearly. It is found in the second part of the judgment God pronounced on Eve: "and thy desire shall be to thy husband and he shall rule over you" (Genesis 3:16 KJV). We must define three key words in the text:

1) desire
2) husband
3) rule

Merriam-Webster's defines *desire* as "a conscious impulse toward something that promises enjoyment or satisfaction in its attainment." According to *Vine's Expository Dictionary of Old and New Testament Words*, the Greek noun for *desire* is *epithumia*, which means "a craving, longing, passion, or turning toward something or someone, both emotionally and sexually." Interestingly enough, the word used for *husband* in the aforementioned passage from Genesis is the Hebrew word *ish*, which is defined as "man, mankind, or husband." The verb *rule* is defined by *Webster's Dictionary* as "the exercise of authority or control." While this is truthful, the accurate Hebrew interpretation of this text suggests that Eve would desire to control her husband in an evil way and that he would have authority over her. As a result of God's pronouncement on Eve, women have a natural urge or passion for men, which is now tainted with evil and must be reversed through prayer and submission to God. Woman's heart, which was originally created for the purest, most innocent love and pursuit of God, was turned toward man, and as a result so is ours.

This is one reason why fathers are so critical during girls' formative years. Women have an innermost craving and longing for the approval of a man; in childhood, it is fulfilled by a healthy relationship with one's father. Girls without the presence of a father in their lives are likely to be more vulnerable to promiscuity, abuse, and low self-esteem. They have a greater struggle with misdirected emotions, having no understanding of the inner need for such a presence. Imagine the magnified misdirection in the life of girls or women who have not only the absence of a father but also no relationship with Jesus Christ, and even more those who are physically or sexually abused or dominated by a man in an unhealthy way during their formative years. As a result, they may gravitate to unhealthy and abusive relationships; feel a need to constantly be with a man; and consequently settle for unsuitable husbands. In many cases, they have never experienced a healthy interaction of any kind with a man, and as a result engage in ineffectual relationships. Interestingly enough, this "turning" described in Genesis 3:16 is so strong, even women who have godly father figures and great father-daughter relationships can fall prey to their desires when they have varied motives and have not fully turned to God.

Have you ever associated with a woman who demonstrates her need to be in a relationship? Could you, perhaps, be one of those women? These are some of the characteristics of such a woman: she is in continual search for relationship, one after the other. Her relationships are often filled with "drama." Perhaps, she never has any relationship at all but often speaks of finding "her husband." In some cases, the woman is married but continually seeks to control her husband through sexual and emotional manipulation. These are all examples of the consequences of misdirected emotions. There is also the woman whose circumstances indicate that she settled for someone other than the one God desired for her. This is the woman who we often judge as "needy," and perhaps it is true. However, the result of Eve's judgment has made us all needy to some degree. You may not be quite as needy as the woman described above. You may be a saved woman who—instead of spending quality time studying, praying, worshipping, and becoming a strong, purposed woman of God—seeks gifts and attention and engages in sexual encounters outside of marriage with "friends" who you manipulate or control. Perhaps you can't identify with this woman either. Maybe you have deeply buried all your desires because of the insecurities, pain, violations, or abuse caused by a man you trusted. Nonetheless, God wants you to experience His healing and not be hindered by the curses on Eve caused by the fall.

What sets these women apart from those, who by the grace of God, conduct themselves differently, is that they have not replaced and fulfilled their innermost longings with a loving and intimate relationship with Christ. God doesn't desire that women operate based on misdirected emotions. To get to the root of our issues, we must expose these behaviors. Many women are plagued with these types of issues and want help.

We must thoroughly examine ourselves and uncover the truth about our behaviors. We have a desire to turn toward man, which must be broken and redirected toward God and an intimate relationship with Jesus Christ, making Him the first husband! He is more than able to fulfill our deepest needs and allow us to walk in the healthy way that may lead to our meeting His choice mate for us, having a completely healed marriage, or being a satisfied single fully dedicated to His purposes. We must understand that this natural desire or turning toward man is born of the flesh and is a result of Eve's actions. As with other flesh-based strongholds and vices, we must fight to correct it, overcome it, and walk in victory. The correction begins with the conscious decision to change; the effort is what is required to overcome those strongholds and to put God in His proper place as Savior, Lord, and King. It is then that we will have the wherewithal to bring the flesh under subjection to His Spirit. When we turn toward God and accept His Lordship, truly allowing Him to be Lord over every area of our lives, He fills the emptiness that appears to exist whether we are with or without a husband. Then we can enjoy victory over misdirected emotions and walk with intentionality as a purposed woman of God in whatever state we find ourselves in.

Married women who have their desires transformed and redirected toward God for fulfillment are much healthier than those who do not. When you are fulfilled by God, your desires toward your spouse are more wholesome, and your expectations more realistic and understanding, in light of who God is, and who your husband is. You see your spouse as *a* friend, provider, leader, protector, and even guide, but not as *the* friend, provider, leader, protector, and guide, consequently giving him room to grow, fail, and feel secure and become even more of the man God desires.

Woman of God, please understand that the revelation in this teaching is null and void if our hearts are not turned back to God. As earlier stated, failure to do this only produces a woman driving a purpose rather than a purposed woman who sees the greatness of our Lord, Savior, and King. See Him high and lifted up as Isaiah declared he saw Him in the year that King Uzziah died (verse 6). When the king died, Isaiah's eyes were truly opened and he saw the Lord in a new and accurate way. Too often there are things in our lives that block us from seeing and obtaining our great God and His purpose for our lives. What in your life is blocking your sight of God and has to die or be removed so you can see and embrace our great God for who He really is? Dethroning those things will help you turn back to the one who has been turned toward you all the while. Use your devotional notes to journal what the Lord reveals to you.

Devotional Notes

Questions

1) How can you ensure that you are not functioning in a broken, needy state as a woman of God? Be quiet before the Lord and ask the Holy Spirit to reveal any hidden areas in which you are not fully dedicated and committed to God first in your life. Write them down, ask for forgiveness, and release them.

2) What can you do to strengthen your intimacy with God as you turn back to Him for the fulfillment that will overflow into every area of your life?

Woman of God, turning and redirecting our emotions back to our Lord is critical. So often, we go through life and obtain successes, but also have issues that rob us of what God has put in our hands. Make the sincere commitment to diligently pursue the things you listed in your devotional notes so you can transform your life. Forget those things that are behind you, and press toward what is ahead. Besides, what you see through your windshield is a lot better than what is in your rearview mirror. Obtain it!

Purposeful Thoughts

Obsession over a man, mankind, society, or having a man is a direct result of being broken, empty, or unfulfilled. You must first acknowledge that God is the only one who can bring healing, meaning, and fulfillment to your life. As long as you try to fill your "God need" with a man, societal status, or other forms of fulfillment, you will never be truly whole or walk in God's purpose for your life. You also will be driven to sustain that fulfillment naturally. If you are married, do not to burden your husband with being what God is intended to be in your life, that is, perfect. Stay in the presence of God, and allow Him to be your all; let your husband be your husband. You will have an improved relationship because the unfair weight to be "everything" will be removed from him. You see him as a great man; yet know he is a man, not the Savior! If you are a single woman believing God for marriage, continue to walk in God's purpose and obey to His word. Delight yourself in Him, and let Him be your greatest desire and joy. Keep your heart submitted to Him, and if it is His will, you will surely find God's choice for your life, but more importantly, he will find you! Be refreshed as you repent, redirect, refocus, and make Christ lord of every area of your life! The Bible instructs us that if we wait on the Lord and be of good courage, He will strengthen our heart. Isn't this a wonderful journey? There is peace and joy on the journey of a purposed woman!

Let's take a look at Genesis 3:23-24, which reveals one of the saddest truths regarding the consequences of misdirected emotions:

> Therefore the LORD God sent him out of the garden of Eden to till the ground from which he was taken. So He drove out the man; and He placed cherubim at the east of the garden of Eden, and a flaming sword which turned every way, to guard the way to the tree of life. (NKJV)

This Scripture reveals something very important about women. Please note that God never required Eve to leave the garden. After God said Adam must not be allowed to take and eat from the tree of life (Genesis 3:22), He expelled him from the garden. Not only did He drive Adam out, He placed an angel and a flaming sword to guard the tree of life from them both.

Genesis 4:1 finds Eve with her husband, after conceiving and giving birth to a son. There is no account that says God allowed Adam to come back into the garden to be with Eve, or that Eve was sent out of the garden, as established is in the preceding verses. This was the first manifestation of God's judgment on Eve: that she would have a desire for her husband, and that he would rule over her.

We know that it was God's ultimate purpose and plan for Adam and Eve to multiply, even in the middle of these circumstances. However, to realize that Eve could and did leave God's presence to be with her husband is a valuable lesson for women. Eve lived in the manifest presence of the almighty God, something that we cannot imagine with any accuracy. Nevertheless, she abandoned His greatness for the comparative futility of Adam. Granted, it is a truth that Adam and Eve were in a union ordained by God, and He indeed had plans for them to be fruitful and multiply; however, the revelation that we must not miss is that we often leave God's presence incomplete to run into what we know to be our purpose, without being restored, ready, or released by God.

This is a poignant illustration of the power of God's judgment on Eve, and its impact on women throughout time. Each day too many of us do the same as Eve did. When we pursue man or the pleasures of mankind rather than our opportunity and privilege to walk in intimacy with God, we are following Adam out of the garden. Many of us follow the ways of mankind, which are isolated from God's presence. The Bible lets us know we cannot serve two masters; we will love one and hate the other. This is one of the worst consequences of misdirected emotions. These truths confirm our need as women to get back to the garden in the presence of God, stop suffering the consequences of misdirected emotions, and allow God's healing hand to restore us. We must remain in our roles as women and not be consumed and influenced by unhealthy emotions, desires, or unaddressed pain. It is critical for women to be whole and balanced, so we can properly assist man and mankind without doing what I call a "187" (slang for homicide or murder), as Eve did by listening to the lies of Satan and responding to her tainted desires. If we maintain our place with God, we will receive the teaching, instructions, and healing that God desires to give us before we make life-altering decisions and before we are released into our purpose.

It is a sad but interesting truth that the first son conceived of this union also had issues with God's sovereignty. Genesis 4:7 contains very similar words as the ones God spoke to Eve; in this case they were repeated to Eve's son, Cain. In chapter 4, Cain is struggling with the rejection of his sacrifice. After speaking to him about his potential to be accepted if he does well, God states that if he doesn't do well, sin (personified) will be waiting at the door (tent post), desiring to rule or master over him. Clearly this is not sexual desire but the desire to control in an evil way. We know that Cain became prey to this desire, which created lifelong consequences from misdirected emotions that, like Eve's, have had an impact on generations to this present day. As we stated, each intimacy produces a seed, and within that seed is the DNA of the mother and father—not only naturally but spiritually. Here, we see a perpetuation of disobedience as well as the same warning to the son of the union of Adam and Eve. This speaks to our need as women to walk in wholeness and obedience, and with intentionality and purpose.

Consider the things that you may be chasing that take you out of the presence of God, and make a sincere commitment to get back in His presence and be developed for His purpose. Maybe that thing is impatience, loss, or shame, or perhaps you are overwhelmed by your situations and circumstances. Let God reverse the consequences of misdirected emotions in your life. Regardless of what you feel, God has great plans for you, and He has always desired to dwell in you: "I am the Lord their God, who brought them up out of the land of Egypt that I may dwell among them. I am the LORD their God" (Exodus 29:46 KJV). "Therefore they are before the throne of God, and serve Him day and night in His temple. And He who sits on the throne will dwell among them" (Revelation 7:15 KJV). Friend, it is God's purpose for us to dwell in His presence. On the road to purpose, be released from every hindrance and distraction, and embrace the love of our true and living purposed God.

Purposeful Thoughts

Women of God, forsake not your King, but rather forsake everything that separates you from His Word, pulls you out of His presence, and takes you off the course of purpose. God loves us and created us to have a true love relationship with Him. He wants to be first in our lives and our hearts' desire, and be the lover of our souls. His desire is that we walk in continual fellowship and friendship with Him. That is awesome! Take a moment to think about it. The great, almighty, true, and living God desires to have a loving relationship with you and me! Consider the great depth of love He has shown toward us. Wow! Each time I ponder on that awesome truth I am reduced to tears. Friend, it is the most exciting and powerful thing that will ever happen to us. Receive the truth of this word, and see yourself as God sees you. He's excited about you, so get excited about Him! The Word of God says that if we draw close to Him, he will draw close to us! Go back to the garden where His warm embrace awaits you. He can dry every tear, heal every hurt, and transform every situation. Walk in victory over every distraction, hindrance, and obstacle to gain more of Him. Woman of God, no longer deny yourself the privilege of such a wonderful, beautiful, and fulfilling relationship, which is guaranteed to change your life for eternity.

Devotional Notes

Women of God, when we consistently walk in the understanding of God's Word, we will be better women, daughters, mothers, sisters, and examples. It is then that we will see the perpetuation of this victorious lifestyle in our children, grandchildren, and their descendants. By God's grace, we can walk in purpose and overcome the consequences of misdirected emotions. Where Eve failed, we can succeed through the power of Jesus Christ and the Holy Spirit, who dwells within us.

Purposeful Points from Chapter 3

1) I will deal with the reality of my emotions, not pretending they do not exist, however, I will direct them toward God to develop the heart and mind of Christ. I curse the "follow your heart" mentality to life, knowing the heart is deceitfully wicked and can't be trusted until it is fully surrendered to God, and shaped into a new heart with pure motives.
2) I will spend quality time with God, worshipping, communicating, and sharing with Him, which will develop my sensitivity to His voice and instructions. I will be more discerning and less likely to fall for the subtle and beguiling tricks of the enemy.
3) I will not give in to the desire to hide or cover up sin. I will expose sin and repent (turn away). The enemy desires for me to stay separated from God, which leads to spiritual death, but I will not allow anything to separate me from my God, Lord, and King.
4) I understand that the natural desire or turning toward man is born of the flesh; therefore, as with other fleshly strongholds and vices, I must fight to correct it, overcome it, and walk in victory. I will keep God in His proper place as Leader, Lord, and King and I will redirect my desires toward Him, bringing the flesh under subjection to His Spirit. As a result, my influence in the lives of others will be blessed and full of life.
5) I will get "back to the garden", under the leadership of God, and be made whole. In the presence of God, I am continually equipped with the teaching, instructions, and healing that is available to me, and as I walk in fellowship with Christ and obedience to His Word, my destiny will embrace me and I will become a purposed woman.

> For the weapons of our warfare are not carnal, but mighty through God to the pulling down of strong holds; Casting down imaginations, and every high thing that exalts itself against the knowledge of God, and bringing into captivity every thought to the obedience of Christ. (2 Corinthians 10:4, 5 KJV)

Chapter 4

In Pursuit of Purpose

In chapters 1 through 3 we examined the biblical truths concerning our unique makeup as women, and the things within women that help shape us for our wonderful, God-intended purpose. The chapters to come will equip you with truths that will help you pursue your specific purpose as it relates to your life. Paul beautifully and simply describes the essence of this pursuit in Philippians 3:12: "not as though I have attained or already been made complete, but that I may lay hold of that for which Christ laid hold of me" (NKJV). There are purposes of God that are specific to you; in order to lay hold of those purposes there are two essentials that you cannot afford to omit:

1) receive your healing
2) pursue the purpose giver

Receive Your Healing

The church today is inundated with more knowledge, teaching, and revelation than ever before. We have been released from the strongholds of various bondages; however, many of us have failed to walk in our deliverance and have become re-entangled. The Bible says in Galatians 5:1: "stand fast therefore in the liberty wherewith Christ has made us free, and be not entangled again with the yoke of bondage" (KJV). It is time that we break our shackles, claim our healing, and walk in wholeness. What comes to mind is the depiction of a chained dog in a large backyard. Over time, he grows accustomed to being stopped by his chain whenever he gets to a certain point. Because he is trained to stay within the boundaries of the chain, when he is released from it, he behaves as though he were still bound by the chain. He will have to be retrained to exercise his newly given freedom.

We are similar in that, through the sacrifice of Jesus Christ, we have been set free from the bondage of sin and death and given authority, dominion, and rights. However, without transformation through the Word of God, we are limited by our former lives and fail to experience the new found liberties available in our life in Christ. The Bible tells us in Romans 12:2: "and do not be conformed to this world, but be transformed by the renewing of your minds that you will prove what is the good and acceptable and perfect will of God" (NKJV). God wants us to be the proof or evidence of what His will is for His people! However, failure to take on a new mindset and walk in that freedom will keep us in a life of stagnancy.

It is imperative that we walk in the healing liberty of Christ. God declares in Exodus 15:26, "For I am the Lord who heals thee" (KJV). God is more than able to heal and deliver us from any type of infirmity, pain, or condition. He can heal every area of our hearts, souls, and spirits. It is a truth that the healing work was accomplished on the cross; however, now we must walk by faith into the manifestation of our healing.

Some of us need physical healing; others need emotional healing; and there are those who are in need of spiritual healing. In every case, healing is essential to victorious living. We often fail to receive and walk in the healing made available to us through Jesus Christ. For the most part, it is not because we lack faith or even doubt God's ability to heal, and it is most definitely not because God can't heal us. In actuality, we are already healed. Everything that is necessary to accomplish our healing has already been done and provided through Christ. In many cases, however, there are essential steps that we fail to accomplish in order to receive the physical, emotional, and spiritual healing and deliverance we so desperately need. Let us explore this further.

In order to *be* healed, we must first acknowledge that we *need* healing. This means we must face the reality that we are distressed and, in some way, suffering. Too often, we fail to acknowledge the reality of our condition, and consequently do not admit or speak the truth about the need for healing or deliverance. We describe positively situations and areas in our lives that are actually a mess.. We even misuse the Scriptures in this effort due to a lack of teaching and understanding. We make statements such as:

1) Well, I'm not going to put my mouth on it [by speaking about it openly].
2) There is life and death in the power of the tongue [so I can't verbally confess my pain].
3) I'm not going to speak it into existence.

Although to some degree, these are valid declarations, we must realize they must be applied appropriately and be relevant to the situation or circumstances. My responses to the above statements and Scriptures, when they are used as clichés, are:

1) If the situation is real, acknowledge it. I mean it's already a reality! God has not instructed us to ignore or avoid reality, but rather has given us the power to walk through and even above it because Christ is in us.
2) Because there is life and death in the power of the tongue, use your tongue to confess the truth about what has occurred. Then profess what the Word of God declares about the situation, and speak life to it!
3) You cannot speak into existence what already exists. If the situation is already bad, it's already a bad situation. If you are already sick, you're sick and are in need of healing! So use your power to speak the reversal of the obvious rather than be afraid to acknowledge its reality and therefore missing your healing.

We must learn to not be so "spiritual" that we operate in "spare rituals," (functioning in spiritual form and fashion but lacking power, or being so heavenly minded that we are no earthly good). Confessing the reality of our situation does not suggest that we doubt God, or even "claim" that the situation is permanent, but rather that we are acknowledging the reality of our needs as well as the source of our healing— Christ. We confess our need with the understanding and confidence that He has already provided our healing and will manifest it naturally. It is not until we acknowledge our true state that the healing and growth process can begin. The pronouncement that the problem exists releases the power of God to work in the situation and, in turn, grows our faith. He touches hearts, minds, and spirits on our behalf. As long as we go on pretending the hurt, pain, and other issues don't exist, we hinder God's work in our situation. If you study the many healing miracles Jesus performed throughout His earthly ministry, you will discover that there were cases in which He prompted the acknowledgement of the need prior to administering healing. No doubt Jesus knew the blind were blind, and the lame were lame; however, in many cases He asked those he healed, what do you need? I believe the fact that the issue was openly stated or known among the people enhanced the miracle. If we go about our daily activities with needs, and fail to go before God in truth, it may appear as if we don't really have a need at all. Some believe that demonstrates faith, but it is quite the contrary. Faith says *this is my issue* and *I believe I am healed* rather than *I don't have an issue* or *Jesus took care of it*. David declared in Psalms 6:2, "Have mercy on me, O Lord, for I am weak; O Lord, heal me, for my bones are troubled" and in Psalms 41:4, "Lord, be merciful to me; heal my soul, for I have sinned against You" (NKJV). It was vital for David to cry out to God repeatedly, transparently, and honestly so he could receive the healing he desperately needed. Isn't that true of us as well?

When we have physical injuries, we immediately do whatever is necessary to bring relief and healing. However, that is not the case with the emotional, mental, and spiritual injuries we sustain, although the same intervention is required. When the hurt first occurs, it seems so much easier to bandage it up and scurry away and assume it will be okay. We often do this, believing the pain of confronting the issue will be greater than the pain caused by the issue. Many of us hate confrontation, and think it is anti-Christian. Perhaps we know that confronting issues may result in feelings resurfacing that have not truly been dealt with, or perhaps we may even fear other undesirable outcomes. Too often, we would rather respond with *I'll pray about it* or *everything will be all right in time*. Often, we fail to realize that the situation may actually worsen with time, perhaps with detrimental consequences. What is amazing is that Jesus gave us the perfect example of when and how to deal with conflict and confront the issues we face. As Christians, we need to understand that some confrontation is healthy and inevitable. To bring healing and resolution, we must learn to express our concerns and deal with issues openly, honestly, wisely and in an appropriate way.

We often pray for God to do the miraculous and give us a testimony. However, we are unwilling to face or uncover the things that are vital to producing that testimony. In other words, we want the testimony without the test. Thinking that we should hold things within us, ignore them, and not deal with painful issues is a trick of the enemy to rob us of the awesome miracles and manifestation of the healing that awaits us. It's time once again to be naked and unashamed, as God created us in the beginning. We do this by exposing ourselves, and then receiving the healing available to us through Christ. When we remove the bandages from our areas of pain, by confession and exposure, we then can allow Jesus to apply the cleansing agent, which is His love, His word, and His promises. He is the great "blotter outer"! Because He loves and cares for us, we can trust Him to cleanse and renew us. In most cases, just like a natural wound, when we are careful not to allow the area to become irritated too soon after healing, we will be made whole and experience true victory and restoration.

I am a true witness of the many physical and emotional healing wonders of God. Today, one could never guess all the sexual, physical, and emotional abuse that caused frequent pain in my life. For years, these things plagued my mind, heart, and spirit, affecting my daily life, even as a believer. Friend, it is because of God's mercy, grace, healing, and redemptive power that I can write these words of life and truth to you. Woman of God, don't you know that our God does not discriminate. What He has done for one, He can do for another. Take the time to write about those damaged areas, and ask the Lord to heal and restore you by the power of the Holy Spirit. Write what comes to mind. What do you see? Woman thou art loosed in Jesus's name!

Devotional Notes

Hope D. Blackwell

Purposeful Thoughts

When a child bumps his or her knee or somehow badly scrapes his or her skin, mothers today will generally do a quick wipe and apply the proper-sized bandage to stop the bleeding and protect the wound from further injury. However, the wiser or older mothers (often the grannies) tell the child, "Let me take that bandage off, and let that wound get some air." They will then apply healing ointment, which, combined with the light and air, will cause full healing to quickly take place. It is the exposure to the light that brings about the healing, and within days the wound will be healed as if nothing had happened. The older women know that bandages are a temporary fix that can stop the bleeding, but will delay the healing.

Incredibly, our spiritual, emotional, and mental healing is not much different. Do you have any wounds that are still covered with bandages that may have stopped the bleeding but have yet to expose the wound to the power of the light and truth found in God's Word? Remove the quick exterior fix, expose those areas, and claim the healing that awaits you! This is the only guarantee for complete and total healing in your life. The Bible declares in Jeremiah 30:17: "'for I will restore health to you and heal you of your wounds,' says the Lord, because they called you an outcast saying: 'This is Zion; No one seeks her'" (NKJV). Well today, God seeks you and desires to be called Jehovah Rophe, your healer. Woman of God, receive your healing!

It is time for women of God to walk in wholeness and healing, free from hurt and pain. For too long we have remained damaged and weak after emotional hurts. The enemy desires to keep us from healing because he knows we will not walk victoriously or effectively without it. Many of us are in bondage due to unforgiveness, jealousy, pride, hatred, envy, and other offenses for which we blame other people or circumstances. These sinful attitudes and strongholds are the center of our pain, and we must be freed from them. The Bible warns us that these things can produce a root of bitterness within us. Woman of God, these are open doors and gateways for demonic intrusion. Hebrews 12:13-15 clearly states:

> And make straight paths for your feet, lest that which is lame be turned out of the way, but let it rather be healed.

> Follow peace with all men, and holiness, without which no man shall see the Lord: Looking diligently lest any man fail of the grace of God; lest any root of bitterness springing up trouble you, and thereby many be defiled. (KJV)

Freedom from these strongholds begins with acknowledgement and confession. The Bible declares: "if we confess our sins, He is faithful and just to forgive our sins, and to cleanse us from all unrighteousness" (1 John 1:9 KJV). Furthermore, we must expose the pain of past disappointments, relationships, financial failure, mistreatment, abuse, hurt, loss, and death. Whatever the source of the pain, it must be acknowledged as the area that needs healing, and we must embrace the love and healing power of God. It is only then that we can begin to live as healthy, purposed women of God, without the baggage of the past and its pains and disappointments. At some point in our lives, we all have all endured some type of pain due to a hurtful or distressing situation and have needed God's hand of healing and restoration. No one is exempt from the need for healing at some point in his or her life, and no one should feel ashamed because of it. God's power will completely heal, renew, and restore you, if you allow Him. Don't impede your path to purpose because of pains from which God desires to release you. Do not hold yourself hostage when God has made you free. The Bible declares: "that He whom the son sets free is truly free indeed" (John 8:36 KJV).

God is calling you to a new place of freedom and fulfillment. He desires to show His glory in your life and use you as an example of His supernatural ability to heal and transform any and every area of brokenness or pain. Woman of God, our God is all powerful, and there is no situation or circumstance beyond His reach. The Bible says, "He giveth power to the faint; and to them that have no might, he increaseth strength" (Isaiah 40:29 KJV). Embrace His power, put on His strength and watch Him move the mountains in your life.

Questions

1) In which areas of your life are you harboring hurt, disappointment, unforgiveness, pride, envy, hate, jealousy, or other areas of pain?

Write down those areas, release them to God, and receive His healing.

> *[handwritten: -am I healed from things w/t? Have I just put them on a back burner?]*

2) Which situations, circumstances, or areas have you ignored in your attempt to avoid a confrontation that God wants you to handle? Remember, some confrontations are necessary for bringing about healing. Search the Scriptures, and see How God's Word instructs us in addressing offenses or confronting people or situations. Ask the Holy Spirit to lead you.

God is a healer and deliverer, and we can cry out to Him in the time of need with confidence that He will hear our cry and answer us. We must declare David's prayer, in Psalms 40:12-17, which reads:

> For innumerable evils have compassed me about: mine iniquities have taken hold upon me, so that I am not able to look up; they are more than the hairs of mine head; therefore my heart faileth me. Be pleased O Lord, to deliver me; O Lord make haste to help me. Let them be ashamed and confounded together that seek after my soul to destroy it; let them be driven backward and put to shame that wish me evil. Let them be desolate for a reward of their shame that say unto me aha, aha. Let all those that seek thee rejoice and be glad in thee: let such as love they salvation say continually, The Lord be magnified. But I am poor and needy; yet the Lord thinketh upon me; thou art my help and my deliverer; make no tarrying, O my God. (KJV)

Get in the face of God, and be honest and transparent. Acknowledge your need for healing, and receive the mercy of God and His grace, which divinely enables us to walk in holiness and health in every area of our lives. Isaiah 57:18-19 states: "I have seen his ways, but I will heal him; I will lead him also and restore comfort unto him and his mourners. I create the fruit of the lips. Peace, peace, to him that is far off, and to him that is near, saith the Lord; and I will heal him" (KJV). Claim your healing today, and embrace the healing and restoration that awaits you. Although God knows and sees our ways, He still desires to grant His forgiveness, peace, and grace to us. There is no God like ours. He is the true and living God.

Pursue the Purpose Giver!

Every person created by God has a purpose, which is only found in the purpose giver. Many never feel the sense of living a truly purposed life because they fail to have a true relationship with the one who gives purpose, our Creator. Even the people who are the most successful, according to the standards of this world, often lack the inner peace and fulfillment that comes from being connected to God and His purpose. Status, wealth, or power will not grant you the joy of walking in sync with the one who created you! In the pursuit of purpose, you must first pursue the purpose giver. There are four foundational steps to building a relationship with the purpose giver. It is vital that these be incorporated in your daily life in order to identify and fulfill your God-ordained purpose. They are:

1) praise
2) worship
3) prayer and communication
4) study of God's Word

Praise

We must fully understand the importance of giving God praise. Psalms 150:6 commands us to "Let everything that hath breath praise the Lord" (KJV). Not only is praise due God because of Who He is, but praise changes our atmosphere as well. As we praise God, we shift our focus totally toward Him, minimizing the attention given to our circumstances, other people, and the enemy. Subsequently, we prepare the atmosphere for God's blessing. We often say, "When the praises go up, the blessings come down"; although that statement is not actually found in Scripture, it is true nonetheless. The Bible does declare that God inhabits the praises of His people. So when we praise God, He actually dwells in our praise, which is with us, and there is no greater blessing than God himself!

No matter who or where you are in life, God deserves the praise. He has the right to be praised, and His worthiness is based on who He is, not who or where you are. This is why He receives praise, and the Bible says, "Let everything that has breath praise the Lord." His command to praise is not restrictive. He said, "everything that has breath"! This is not based upon age, status, or even relationship. This type of praise is the acknowledgement of our maker, which, as stated, is a command. The Bible declares that if we fail to do this, even the rocks will praise Him. We have been created and chosen to praise Him. The Bible states in 1 Peter 2:9: "You are a chosen generation, a royal priesthood, an holy nation, a peculiar people; that ye should show forth the praises of Him who hath called you out of darkness into His marvelous light" (KJV). If the awesomeness of who God is does not compel you to praise Him, at least those who have been brought out of darkness into the light of new life in Christ should easily issue the praises of God! Unfortunately, many praise Him primarily for what He has done, not for who He is. That is the "I'm looking for my breakthrough" praise. This is why praise often appears to be an emotionalism linked to a blessing or the WIFM (what's in it for me) mentality. God demonstrates throughout Scripture his frustration with this type of praise.

This is validated in 1 Samuel 4:5, 6, which states:

> When the ark of the covenant of the Lord came into the camp all Israel shouted with a great shout, so that the earth rang again. When the Philistines heard the noise of the shout they said, "What meaneth the noise of this great shout in the camp of the Hebrews?" And they understood that the ark of the Lord was come into the camp. (KJV)

What is interesting in the Scripture is that it states that the earth, not heaven, rang again. Their shouting didn't get the attention of God or heaven, but of the men who were on earth. The Scripture even states that the Philistines didn't hear the sound of the shout, but the noise of it. It was not an authentic shout of true praise, and the Lord was not moved by it. It was religious enthusiasm and emotionalism with no power, because the Israelites were void of His presence and reverence for who He is. They shouted upon the entry of the Ark of the Covenant, with hopes that with the ark in their midst, God would be with them and give them victory. They released a shout to deceive their enemies into thinking that there was something to it. They wanted them to know, *We have the ark! God is with us to fight for us!* However, they didn't have the presence of God. They were so warped in their image of God, lacking true love and intimacy with Him, they could not see that the ark's presence alone could not atone for their evil nor guarantee the presence of God.

This type of praise is often what the unsaved see and resist. They see people who praise and shout, yet live a lifestyle filled with disobedience and carnality. They see praise motivated by emotionalism and selfishness that ends when the blessing doesn't appear to come in time, that is, our time! In other words, we are offering a conditional praise for a blessing, breakthrough, or deliverance and not because of love and passion for God and excitement about who He is and who we are in Him! This kind of praise must be matured if we ever really want the presence, peace, and full power of God. We must begin to authentically praise God, to see Him for who He is, not merely what He does.

Purposeful Thoughts

God wants you to praise Him as more than Jireh, your provider, Shalom, your peace, or Rophe, your healer. Although He is "all that", He is so much more! You must go beyond the praise for what He does, and praise Him for who He is. Praise Him because of His sovereignty. He is Adonai, Lord Master and El Shaddai, Lord God Almighty! He is the creator of heaven and earth, God of the whole earth, the alpha and omega, the author and finisher of our faith, the sovereign God, King of Kings, Lord of Lords, and the King of all glory. Make a commitment in the pursuit of a purposed life to praise the Lord with reverence and understanding.

Questions

What are ways that you can develop the attitude and posture of continual praise?

Praising Him opens the door to His presence. However, there is a major obstacle to fulfilling purpose: after we have gained access to Him through our praise and thanksgiving, that's as far as many of us go. We deprive ourselves of the continual presence of God, of Him dwelling among us. When we stop at praise, we stop the pursuit of purpose, because victory over the flesh and transformation of the mind and will occur in both praise and worship. Praise is the first step in our pursuit, and it should guide us into the second step, which is worship.

Worship

Worship is quite different than praise. Everyone is commanded to give God praise, which is the acknowledgement and affirmation of His greatness. However, the Bible clarifies that " . . . they that worship Him must worship Him in spirit and in truth" (John 4:24 KJV). When we worship God, it is not linked to a blessing, praise report, song, or emotional gesture. We are provoked by our understanding of the sovereignty of God and who He is in all of His glory. When we worship the Lord in the beauty of holiness (1 Chronicles 16:30), it is with the knowledge of who He is and the desire to know Him in an even deeper, more intimate way. To worship God in spirit and truth is to first recognize that our spirits were created to worship God and long to accomplish that.

Moreover, it is imperative that we fully understand that we cannot truly worship Him in falsehood and deceit, but only in the truth of who He is. Unlike praise, which draws God into our atmosphere, worship escorts us into His presence, a realm where we can only stand in awe of His glory and His greatness. Our flesh decreases in the midst of a daily lifestyle of worship. Every lie, unholy thought, attitude, emotion, and unacceptable spirit within us is exposed as we get into His presence and dwell there. When you develop a lifestyle of worship, a deeper experience with God takes place. During times of praise, your atmosphere changes. In worship you and your innermost being change. This happens as a result of being continually in the presence of the perfect, holy, all-wise, and all-knowing God. It was not until Isaiah saw and acknowledged the Lord for who He was that he declared himself undone and unclean. When we revere God, He exposes us, and in turn we get purged intimately in His glorious presence. In essence, true worship becomes a life in His presence.

Worship is not merely the songs we sing, though they are beautiful and vital. It is not confined to some goose-bump experience, and it certainly cannot be defined by a designated "worship time." It is a lifestyle of love, reverence, adoration, and surrender, with the understanding that we are continually in the presence of our most Holy God in everything we do, that we are in Him, and He dwells within us! Don't misunderstand the term "get in the presence of God," which does not suggest that we aren't continually in His presence. This expression is often used to describe a time of retreat away from everything, in total and complete focus on God. A true worshipper is in a continual mode of worship, carrying His presence everywhere because He is dwelling in us, and there is continual communion. The Bible states in 1 Corinthians 3:16: "Know ye not that your body is the temple of the God, and the Spirit of God dwells in you?" We are carriers of the spirit of God, and as such our worship must go beyond walls, words, and expressions and must be the complete and total lifestyle we live in honor and reverence of the living God.

The leadership of God and His blessings are discovered in worshipful living. In worship and adoration is where we fully see and embrace the divine nature and character of almighty God. David recognized that it was in God's presence that he would be led through life and discover the fullness of joy and true blessing. He states in Psalms 16:11: "You will show me the path of life; In Your presence is fullness of joy; At Your right hand are pleasures forevermore" (NKJV). What is so amazing is that when you worship God with the intent of blessing and honoring Him, you too are blessed, as David discovered. This speaks to the giving nature of God. There is a joy that is released through worship, because in the presence of God, I am overwhelmed by the joy that this great God desires to spend time with me! It is awesome. He is your love, and you are His too. Wow! It is the most beautiful and perfect love relationship and can only be experienced with Christ. It is actually indescribable. God went through great lengths to be in this relationship and fellowship with us. The very least that we can do is worship Him! We were created to worship and adore Him. The Bible says in Romans 12:1 that we "by the mercies of God" should present ourselves as a "living sacrifice, holy, acceptable unto God." This is our reasonable service or spiritual worship. So the true essence of worship is to give Him our whole self at all times. Ask God to open up your understanding of worship, and begin to see worship as a lifestyle that is a joy and not an action. Remember, John 4:23, 24 states: "But the hour cometh, and now is, when the true worshippers shall worship the Father in spirit and in truth: for the Father seeketh such to worship him. God is a Spirit and they that worship Him must worship Him in Spirit and in truth" (KJV). Again, we must worship God in the truth and understanding of who He is, and who we have been made in Him—spirits united with Him through Christ.

Purposeful Thoughts

We often experience visitations from God. However, God desires a habitation, a place where He can dwell and be worshipped at all times. Make a commitment to become a true dwelling place of God. When you think about preparing your home for a new resident, especially someone you love and are excited about, naturally you want to fill your home with things that will be inviting and comforting. You pick up the new things, get rid of the old things, and clean up "white glove" style! Consider that the awesome, true, and living God wants to come and dwell in your earthly tabernacle. What can you do to make Him welcome? What do you need to pick up, get rid of, or clean up? Ask Him for the strength to help you prepare for His residence. Let us declare the words of Jesse Dixon from his song, Lord Prepare Me to be a Sanctuary: "Lord prepare me to be a sanctuary, pure and holy, tried and true; and with thanksgiving, I'll be a living sanctuary, Lord for you!"

Questions

What are ways in which you can develop the attitude and posture of continual worship?

God is looking for pure worship, and a purposed woman whose heart belongs to Him. The Bible makes us aware in 2 Chronicles 16:9 that " . . . the eyes of the Lord run to and fro throughout the whole earth, to show himself strong in the behalf of them whose heart is perfect toward him" (KJV). God is searching for that woman of worship and purpose through whose life He can be glorified.

Prayer and Communication

Just as praise guides us into worship, worship escorts us into a deeper level of prayer and communication with God. In the pursuit of purpose, prayer is the key that unlocks doors in our lives and the lives of others. When we say prayers of thanksgiving, make professions of faith in God's promises, declare His Word, and confidently and thankfully make known our requests, God opens His more than sufficient hand to us and answers our prayers. The Bible teaches us in Philippians 4:6 that we should be anxious for nothing but by prayer and supplication, with thanksgiving, make our requests to God. The peace of God, which surpasses all understanding, will guard our hearts and minds in Christ Jesus. It is God's will for us to communicate with Him in prayer about *everything*. He is ready to release His peace and comfort to us, which is why prayer and communication go hand in hand. Prayer is the language by which we communicate with God. When we pray, He responds each time in some way.

Prayer also allows us to exercise our God given authority to change lives and circumstances on the earth. Matthew 16:19 states: "I will give you the keys to the kingdom of heaven, and whatever you bind on earth will be bound in heaven, and whatever you loose on earth will be loosed in heaven" (NIV"). Let us go back to the garden for a moment.

Genesis 1:26-27 indicates that God gave man dominion over all the earth: everything in it and everything associated with it. This means we have authority and control over the affairs of the earth. It is when we pray that we invite God into those affairs, knowing that apart from Him we are powerless and can do nothing. This is why it is important for us to utilize the most powerful weapon of warfare, which is prayer. As stated in Matthew 16:19, it is prayer and declaration that causes us to operate in the heavenly realm, creating the will of heaven on earth for the manifestation of God's purposes, which we have the ability to pray into existence.

Further validation of this is found in 2 Chronicles 7:14, 15: "If My people who are called by My name will humble themselves, and pray and seek My face, and turn from their wicked ways, then I will hear from heaven, and will forgive their sin and heal their land. Now My eyes will be open and My ears attentive to prayer *made* in this place" (NKJV). This is God's way of saying, *I'll get involved in the matters of my people on earth, when they repent, recognize their need for me, communicate with me through prayer, and live holy lives.* Remember, God gave us dominion over the affairs of this world. We must now demonstrate our reliance on Him through prayer and declarations that line up with His Word and His will. To go without prayer and continual communication with God is to shut down your connection to the power source necessary for your existence as a believer. It is like cutting off the oxygen supply to someone on life support. I can't imagine why someone who professes to be in relationship with God would not pray or communicate with the one they love. Prayer is the primary means of communication with God. The Bible declares in James 5:16 that the "effective, fervent prayer of a righteous man avails much" (NKJV). God hears your prayers, and that communication intensifies your relationship with Him. Not only do you speak to Him, but He speaks to you and gives you peace and direction for your life!

Purposeful Thoughts

Without the communication of both partners, a marriage will suffer. The relationship will be dull, creating distance between the two. No matter how much one spouse tries to talk, if the other fails to reciprocate, the relationship will be strained and therefore will not function in its full potential. The spouse that longs to share is unable to do so because of the silence of the other.

Similarly, when you withhold prayer and honest communication from God—despite how much He desires to show you, tell you, or share—you are blocking the primary channel of communication. Yes, He knows all and can do all, but prayer is the primary channel of communication that must be used for you to hear from Him, receive instructions, understand, and implement His Word. It is imperative that you initiate communication and dialogue with God and have an ear to hear what He is saying to you. Make a commitment to share your heart, time, desires, and most difficult issues with God in prayer.

We must have two-way communication with God, whereby we not only pray, but listen to Him as He responds. He responds primarily through His Word (the Bible), circumstances, and people. We must be real with God, honest, and transparent in our prayers and communication with Him. Proverbs 15:8 states: "The sacrifice of the wicked is hateful and exceedingly offensive to the Lord, but the prayer of the upright is his delight" (AB).

The Bible further instructs us in Jeremiah 29:12-14:

> Then you will call upon Me and go and pray to Me, and I will listen to you. [It is our prayers that get His attention and causes Him to listen to us.] And you will seek Me and find Me, when you search for Me with all your heart. [We have to seek Him diligently in prayer, openly and with everything that is in us.] Then, I will be found by you, says the Lord, and I will bring you back from your captivity; I will gather you from all the nations and from all the places where I have driven you, says the Lord, and I will bring you to the place from which I cause you to be carried away captive. [He promises to not only listen, but to make Himself available to us in prayer and move on our behalf.] (NKJV)

What a wonderful promise, to know that God will listen and be available to you when you avail yourself to Him, and seek Him with everything within you. It is then that God moves in our lives in extraordinary ways. I am truly a witness to this. Commit yourself to having more open and honest talks with God. Share your feelings, pains, struggles, and confess your need for more of Him. Receive His love, His word, the ministry of the Holy Spirit, and let Him speak to your heart; then make a conscious commitment to obey. Start with your devotional notes.

Devotional Notes

Questions

1) How can you make more time for prayer and communication with God? How can you make the time you share with God more rewarding?

2) What are some common hindrances to your developing a more disciplined prayer life?

God had a purpose for you even before your conception. Prayer, communication, and diligently seeking God are critical to revealing that purpose. Once again, meditate on the scripture in Jeremiah 29:11-13, which so beautifully sums up our study on prayer and communication:

> For I know the thoughts that I think toward you, says the Lord, thoughts of peace and not of evil, to give you a future and a hope. Then you will call upon Me and go and pray to

Me and I will listen to you. And you will seek Me and find Me, when you search for me with all your heart. (NKJV)

Study of God's Word

Prayer and communication go hand-in-hand with the study of the Word of God. John 15:7 states, "if you abide in me and my word abides in you, ask what you will and it shall be done unto you" (KJV). This leads us to the fourth step in the pursuit of purpose, which is the study of God's Word.

It is the Word living within us that causes God to grant our petitions. If God's Word truly dwells within us, we will pray according to His will. We will communicate with Him just as Jesus did. We must plant the Word of God deep within our hearts. If we fail to study the Word, we will not have the weapons necessary for destroying our three greatest enemies; the flesh, world systems, and the devil. We must constantly feed our spirits the Word of God in order to be strong enough to combat the lusts of the flesh (carnal-sin nature). Like David, we must hide God's Word in our hearts so that we will not sin against Him. The only way that can be accomplished is through study and meditation. It is the truth of His Word that will defeat and destroy the lies of Satan as well as every false imagination that exalts itself against Christ. When Jesus was tempted by Satan, he walked in authority by releasing the Word. If the Word is not in us, we have nothing to release, which makes us powerless.

The Bible instructs us in 2 Timothy 2:15 to study to show ourselves approved unto God." It further indicates that a workman (i.e., one of us), need not to be ashamed when correctly handling and understanding the Word of truth. To correctly handle the Word is to be skilled in the Word and to walk in understanding and accuracy. This is only achieved with intense study and revelation by the Holy Spirit. David says much about God's Word that reflects his dependence on its power in his life. He shares throughout the book of Psalms: "I hope in thy Word. I meditate on thy Word. I am quickened by thy Word. I hide thy Word in my heart. I'm in awe of thy Word." Friend, God's Word is truly our daily bread. We need it to live. The Word strengthens our faith and causes us to have an ear to hear and further know Him. The Word is how we know God's will for our lives. The Bible says in

Romans 10:17, "So then faith comes by hearing, and hearing by the Word of God" (KJV). It is essential that we dissect this verse. Our faith is developed by our hearing the Word, and our ability to hear is also developed by the Word. Just as prayer is our primary means of communication with God, His Word is often the method He uses to speak to us. David said in Psalms 119:105, "Thy word is a lamp unto my feet and a light unto my path" (KJV). His Word directs us, guides us, and illuminates the way for us. Without His Word, we would not know His will for us or have the wisdom, ability, or understanding to navigate through our purposed journey on earth.

Questions

1) What are ways in which you can enhance your study of the Word of God?

2) What are common hindrances to your having a consistent and effective devotional life? Think of ways to push through those barriers, and let the love of God motivate you.

3) Write down the areas in your life that lack direction. Search the Scriptures to see what His Word says about them. Release these areas to God, and make a commitment to obey Him.

To be women of purpose, we must claim our healing and pursue the purpose giver. These are major components in the pursuit of purpose.

When we receive our healing and pursue the purpose giver, we will inevitably walk in purpose.

Woman of God, how can you walk with God daily in a relationship, seeking His truths without obtaining His purposes, plans, and promises for your life? Paul said these powerful words in Philippians 3:12-17 as it relates to the pursuit of purpose:

> It's not that I have already reached this goal or have already been perfected, but I pursue it, so that I may grab hold of it because Christ grabbed hold of me for just this purpose. Brothers and sisters, I myself don't think I've reached it, but I do this one thing: I forget about the things behind me and reach out for the things ahead of me. The goal I pursue is the prize of God's upward call in Christ Jesus. So, all of us who are spiritually mature should think this way and if anyone thinks differently, God will reveal it to him or her. Only let's live in a way that is consistent with whatever level we have reached. Brothers and sisters become imitators of me and watch those who live this way—you can use us as models. As I have told you many times and now say with deep sadness, many people live as enemies of the cross. Their lives end with destruction. Their god is their stomach, and they take pride in their disgrace because their thoughts focus on earthly things. Our citizenship is in heaven. We look forward to a savior that comes from there—the Lord Jesus Christ. He will transform our humble bodies so that they are like his glorious body, by the power that also makes him able to subject all things to himself. (CEB)

Friend, as you pursue God, you become a light and compass to others, providing instruction and even direction. Don't you want your declaration to be as Paul so assuredly says, "Brothers and sisters become imitators of me and watch those who live this way—you can use us as models"! What dedication he possessed. I challenge you to seize the purpose of God for your life, which is found when you lay hold of the purpose giver, and let Him strengthen you spiritually, mentally, emotionally, and naturally.

Beloved, I pray above all else that you will prosper in all things and be in health, even as your soul prospers. In your devotional notes, write about various types of healing in your life as well as areas that you are believing for your healing to manifest. Search out the Word of God and the many promises He has made to those who trust Him and stand on His Word without wavering. Fully trust God to bring you to a new place of wholeness as you pursue Him, and embrace His Word and His wonderful plans and purpose for your life. Remember, the Word of God declares that He has good plans for you, plans that will give you a hope and a future. No matter how things seem, those plans shall prevail. Woman of God, this is the journey of the truest of purposed women. I believe you are in pursuit of purpose.

Devotional Notes

Purposeful Points from Chapter 4

1) To *be* healed, I must first acknowledge my *need* for healing. This means I must face the reality that I am distressed or in need. Too often, in situations, I fail to acknowledge the reality of my condition; consequently, I do not admit the truth about my need for healing or deliverance. I will change these behaviors, claim my healing, and receive my deliverance.
2) Many of us are in bondage due to unforgiveness, jealousy, pride, hatred, envy, and other poisonous issues. These sinful emotions and attitudes are the center of our pain, and we must be freed from them. We accomplish this by confessing our sins. The Bible declares in 1 John 1:9 that "if we confess our sins, He is faithful and just to forgive our sins, and to cleanse us from all unrighteousness" (KJV). I will honestly release the people or circumstances associated with my pain, and walk in health in every area of my life.
3) I will strengthen my relationship with God and pursue Him through praise and worship. I will do as Philippians 4:8 states: "whatever things are true, whatever things are noble, whatever things are just, whatever things are pure, whatever things are lovely, whatever things are of good report, if there is any virtue and if there is anything praiseworthy, meditate on these things" (NKJV).
4) In the pursuit of God, I will develop a lifestyle of continual prayer and communication, with confidence that the effectual and fervent prayers of the righteous accomplish much.
5) I will commit to reading, studying, and meditating on God's Word. This will lead me to the place where I can know, understand, and live in the purpose of God for my life.

> Come, and let us return unto the Lord: for He hath torn, and He will heal us; He hath smitten, and He will bind us up. (Hosea 6:1 KJV)

Chapter 5

Called to Conquer

> And I will put enmity between you and the woman, and between your offspring and hers; he shall crush your head and you shall strike his heel. (Genesis 3:15 NIV)

As a woman of purpose, you must recognize that you have been called to conquer. You have been given victory through Jesus Christ over every evil work. Therefore, you can take the purposed journey, as well as the blows of the enemy, with a special confidence. Woman of God, you have overcome before you even enter the storm, and you have won before you even step onto the frontlines of battle! There are three revelations in this chapter that will birth in you a newfound freedom to walk with confidence as more than a conqueror:

1) the hatred within
2) the promise
3) His Word to you

The Hatred Within

The first portion of our reference passage, found in Genesis 3:14 reads: " . . . and I will put enmity between you and the woman, between your offspring and hers . . ." *Enmity* can be defined as mutual hatred or ill will. *Vine's Expository Dictionary of Old and New Testament Words* lists the Hebrew word for enmity as *echthra*, meaning "hostility" or "opposition." It is vital that we understand the purpose for this intense opposition or hatred that was originally instituted by God in the Garden of Eden.

It is important that we recognize the effects of our trials and tests. In the garden, Eve dealt with the enemy head on. Undoubtedly, she played a role in their demise, which occurred because of her communication with the enemy; however, that does not negate the fact that she was deceived by him. Subsequently, she possessed the ability to identify the serpent as a deceiver. When we have encounters with the enemy that we recognize, our discernment should be sharpened and our ability to expose him should increase, as if we were exercising a physical muscle. This is how we grow in spiritual things. Hebrews 5:14 states that "strong meat belongs to those of full age, even those who by reason of use have their senses exercised to discern both good and evil" (KJV). It is our responsibility to grow as we victoriously deal with the enemy and also when we are not so victorious!

We know Eve didn't walk in authority over the serpent, but we do know that God in His great love and mercy covered Adam and Eve after their fall. Yes, in their disobedience they were left ashamed, exposed, uncovered, and stripped of all the wonderful privileges originally given by God. But God removed their false coverings, and through the first sacrifice (the shedding of a blood of an animal), He provided them with adequate coverings. This was an example of what was to come for us. Through their disobedience, we were born into sin. But through God's sacrifice of Jesus Christ and the shedding of His blood on Calvary, we were covered and put back in right standing with God as well as given the power to overcome all of Satan's subtle and crafty tricks. Unlike Eve, once we have fallen prey to the traps of the enemy and exercised the victory we have through Christ, we should develop a greater passion to defeat the enemy and crush his head (or authority), as promised in Scripture. This passion or fuel to destroy him is derived from the hatred God put in us for the enemy in the beginning. The enmity or "hatred within" is designed for the enemy, not for people! The enemy knows whether or not we truly hate him, or will entertain him. When that hatred was placed between the serpent and the woman, it was mutual, not one-sided, as we have been lulled into thinking and acting. However, we must remember that Satan and the kingdoms of darkness are in direct opposition of God and His kingdom. The Bible says that we cannot serve two masters; either we will hate the one and

aim hate towards the enemy

Hope D. Blackwell

love the other, or we will hold to the one and despise the other. When we are reminded of the enemy's hatred for us and great efforts to cause a break in fellowship between us and our loving and merciful God, it should be easy to choose which to hate. That hatred should become a motivator to walk in victory over him, just as much as our love for God and His kingdom does.

Purposeful Thoughts

Ladies, wake up! We are to hate the enemy as much as he hates us. Our hatred is the fuel that will fire us up enough to identify, expose, and destroy the evils of Satan, his followers, and his hierarchy of spiritual wickedness. This is why it is essential to claim our healing and deliverance, and then turn our hearts back to God, so we can take out the right enemy and not innocent bystanders. We must develop a love for the things and people of God, so that our only hatred will be for the one for whom it was originally intended—Satan. We must annihilate his attempts to kill, steal, and destroy. Are you continually locked in a "ready, aim, and fire" mode, unleashing the hatred within you onto the enemy? Make a commitment to use wisdom, and do not let the hatred within be unleashed on the people you were designed to protect. This is a trap that awaits us, but we are victorious!

If we are not tuned in to Christ and led by the Spirit of God, we will release the hatred and opposition that was put within us onto people, instead of onto the demonic influence of Satan that it is intended to destroy. Without healing and spiritual development through prayer, worship, and study, we will have distorted and inaccurate natural and spiritual insights. This will impair our ability to see, causing us to identify the wrong targets, fire inaccurately and destroy those we were designed to help, assist, and protect. This misfiring is similar to the broken rib mentioned in chapter 1, which punctures in a broken state as opposed to protecting in a healed state. As previously stated, in its broken condition, the rib has the power to annihilate the very things it was designed to protect.

God has uniquely designed the woman to wage natural and spiritual battles. Although we are physically more fragile than men, we have the ability to endure as many, if not more, challenges, changes, discomfort, and pain in frequency and intensity. We know this even by the way our bodies are designed for childbirth, as mentioned in chapter 3. We can imagine that Adam, who was the head, may have walked throughout the garden without being aware that there was an enemy lurking about. You must remember that the woman is called the helpmeet or suitable helper. It remains our responsibility to be "fruit inspectors," to not release anything, anywhere, to anyone that doesn't line up with the Word and will of God. It is clear that Adam didn't question what Eve gave him and that he was right there with her in the process of her deception (Genesis 2:6: " . . . and gave also to her husband, who was with her"). While this speaks of many things, I believe it speaks volumes of the level of trust, dependency, and confidence that Adam originally had in Eve and her choices and assistance. Obviously, Adam was depending on Eve to give him what he needed and what was good for him. Purposed woman, it is "time out" for failing our Adams of today. We must walk in our victory, and conquer the enemy of our souls!

We have a great responsibility as helpers in our marriages, families, churches, communities, and businesses as well as to future generations. We have to understand the enemy hates us, and it is our job to hate and destroy him. He knows who we are, who we represent, and that we have the power within us to destroy him. However, we must be equally aware of these truths. Understand the hatred within, and don't allow the enemy to "play" you, as he did Eve. It is your responsibility to be a good steward over everything God has entrusted to you as well as everything He has entrusted you to do.

Ask yourself these questions, and let the Holy Spirit show you the true answers: How can I be a better helper to those around me and ensure that the enemy's influence is limited in my life and the lives of others? In what areas do I have a tendency to "misfire" onto others? Why? Think of ways to see God glorified in your life as you embrace this powerful revelation!

Questions

Think of times that you felt "the hatred within" and knowingly (or unknowingly) directed those emotions and feelings to the wrong enemy, leaving someone hurt in the process. How can you avoid this in the future and ensure that it is the enemy who is exposed and destroyed?

Three passages from Scripture in the book of Revelation confirm the existence of this enmity and validate the prophetic scripture in Genesis 3:14, 15:

> So the Lord God said to the serpent: "Because you have done this, you are cursed more than all cattle, and more than every beast of the field; on your belly you shall go, and you shall eat dust all the days of your life. And I will put enmity between you and the woman, and between your seed and her Seed; He shall bruise your head, and you shall bruise His heel." (NKJV)

These powerful scriptures also confirm our preordained victory over the enemy, through Jesus Christ.

> And there appeared a great wonder in heaven; a woman clothed with the sun, and the moon under her feet, and upon her head a crown of twelve stars. And she being with child cried, travailing in birth, and pained to be delivered . . . and his tail drew the third part of the stars of heaven, and did cast them down to the earth: and the dragon stood before the woman which was ready to be delivered, for to devour her child as soon as it was born. (Revelation 12:1, 2, 4 KJV)

> And when the dragon saw that he was cast unto the earth, he persecuted the woman which brought forth the man child. (Revelation 12:13 KJV)

> And the dragon was wroth with the woman, and went to make war with the remnant of her seed, which keep the commandments of God and have the testimony of Jesus Christ. (Revelation 12:17 KJV)

These scriptures make us aware that Satan will be on the heels of believers to attempt to steal, kill, and destroy the purposes and promises of God for our lives. We must realize that while he and his cohorts are on our heels, according to the powerful scripture in Genesis 3:15, that is as far as they can go! So while we grasp the understanding that Satan is and will be after us, as with any war or mutual opposition, we should pursue him just as aggressively. We must fight this fight with proven spiritual weapons. The Bible instructs us in 2 Corinthians 10:3-6:

> ... though we live in the world we do not wage war as the world does. The weapons we fight with are not the weapons of this world. On the contrary, they have the divine power to demolish strongholds. We demolish arguments and every pretension that sets itself up against the knowledge of God and we take captive every thought to make it obedient to Christ. And we will be ready to punish every act of disobedience, once your obedience is complete. (NIV)

We must operate in faith and put on the whole armor of God, which is found in Ephesians 6:10-20:

> Finally, my brethren, be strong in the Lord and in the power of His might. Put on the whole armor of God that you may be able to stand against the wiles of the devil. For we do not wrestle against flesh and blood, but against principalities, against powers, against the rulers of the darkness of this age, against spiritual hosts of wickedness in the heavenly places. Therefore take up the whole armor of God that you may be able to withstand in the evil day, and having done all, to stand. Stand therefore, having girded your waist with truth, having put on the breastplate of righteousness, and having shod your feet with the preparation of the gospel of peace; above all, taking the shield of faith with which you will be able to quench all the fiery darts of the wicked one. And take the helmet of salvation, and the sword of the Spirit, which is the word of God; praying always with all prayer and supplication in the Spirit, being watchful to this end with all perseverance and supplication for all the saints—and for me, that utterance may be given to me, that I may open my mouth boldly to make known the mystery of the gospel, for which I am an ambassador in chains; that in it I may speak boldly, as I ought to speak. (NKJV)

We must know God and His word!

Hope D. Blackwell

As a purposed woman who is called to conquer, you must comprehend the two parts of this Scripture that require more specific concentration. The first are "the wiles" or trickery of the devil, which we dissected in chapter 2, "The Thief of Purpose." These wiles are the deceitful and beguiling strategies of the enemy meant to steal, kill, and destroy your purpose in Christ. To stand against them, you must be filled with the truth of God's Word and His spirit. With each generation, more subtle and crafty schemes are released from the pit of hell. To overcome, we must know God and His Word.

The second portion is "the evil day," the time in which we now live, when, all over the world, hell is breaking loose in our communities, societies, and governments. The Word of God gives us direction, for navigating through these times victoriously. We must stand up, square our shoulders, and go to battle with confidence. This, my friend, is the only way that we will reign victorious in battle in such days as these. We must understand this is a war filled with hatred and opposition, but the Word of God promises us power and victory through Jesus Christ. It is important for us to fully comprehend that Satan is truly trampled under our feet. With our own mouths, we often give him too much credit and power. Purposed woman, get prepared for battle by embracing the Word of God that declares: "God has given you power to tread on serpents and scorpions, and over all the power of the enemy: and nothing shall by any means hurt you" (Luke 10:19 KJV).

Questions

In what ways can you help the next generation understand the principle of the hatred within to ensure that they know the real enemy and are well equipped for battle in these last and evil days that lie ahead?

The Purposed Woman

Devotional Notes

The Promise

The second portion of our referenced passage in Genesis 3:14 reads, " . . . he shall bruise your head and you shall bruise his heel" (NKJV). Woman of God, be reminded that the promise is victory. From Genesis through Revelation, God promises us victory in every battle. Our previous Scripture passage described the war between Satan and believers and our promised victory through Christ Jesus. Remember that God loves us so much that, despite the crime committed against Him in the garden, He still had a great and mighty plan for us. The enemy used mankind, specifically a woman, as the vehicle for bringing sin into the world. God, in His mercy, omnipotence, grace, and compassion, used the same vehicle (a woman) to birth the cure that would rectify sin—Jesus Christ. In the midst of God's judgment on Eve and Adam, He extended the opportunity in which our relationship with Him could be restored, knowing that our reconciliation would be vital in the war with Satan. Even with our imperfections, God desires that we walk in the power and anointing and be more than conquerors. What an awesome God we serve. Glory to His name!

Let's examine what God is saying to us in this passage: " . . . he shall bruise your head and you shall bruise his heel." The "he" God is referring to is the seed of the woman, Jesus Christ. Through the birth, death, resurrection, and ascension of Jesus Christ, the enemy's head (which speaks to his authority) shall be bruised, or crushed (as it is translated in Hebrew), which means inoperable or destroyed. The only recourse that the enemy has is permission to strike Christ's heel, that is, His earthly walk. This speaks to Satan's ability to challenge Christ; however, it also means that this is all he will be permitted to do—not only to Christ, the seed of the woman, but to every seed to follow, which includes every believer who has faith in Christ.

Woman of God, as an heir of Christ, you have been given the power to crush the head (authority) of the enemy on the earth (i.e.,

Hope D. Blackwell

[Handwritten margin notes: "We must live in obedience to experience continued victory!" and "We must work at obeying to remain conquerors"]

your life and the lives of others, businesses, governments, and world systems). The most the enemy is permitted to do to you is strike your heel, which again, speaks to the occasional pains or challenges he may devise for you. However, you will remain victorious through Christ! A strike to the heel may slow you down occasionally, but it doesn't rule you out or stop you. He does not have the power to destroy you unless you give him that access. Remember, Satan was cursed in the Garden of Eden to roam around and "eat dust," which speaks to flesh and the carnality of the outer man. He is only given more authority when you open the door through sin, disobedience, and the works of the flesh, which invite him into your life for future destruction. Romans 8:36, 37 states: "For your sake we face death all day long; we are considered as sheep to be slaughtered. No, in all these things we are more than conquerors through him that loved us" (NIV). Dear sister, even when you feel that you have been slaughtered by life and maybe even the enemy, remember the promise of God is that you are still a conqueror through Jesus Christ.

Questions

1) How can you crush the authority of the enemy in your life, marriage, family, business, and community?

   By remaining faithful, seeking him wholeheartedly

2) What are some "strikes to the heel" that may have slowed you down in your walk with Christ? How did you overcome those times?

If we examine a few other scriptural passages, found in the book of Revelation, another remarkable fact is revealed. As we have examined the hatred and the war, let's now study the promises revealed in the following passages:

> . . . the woman fled into the wilderness where she hath a place prepared of God, that they should feed her there a thousand two hundred and threescore days. (Revelation 12:6 KJV)

> And they overcame him by the blood of the lamb and by the word of their testimony, and they loved not their lives unto the death. (Revelation 12:11 KJV)

> And to the woman were given two wings of a great eagle that she might fly into the wilderness, into her place, where she is nourished for a time, and times, and half a time from the face of the serpent. (Revelation 12:4 KJV)

These Scriptures are the revelation of things to come in the war between God and Satan, between the people of God and the prince of this world, the devil. In verse 6, the wilderness represents a place of refuge and protection (unlike most of the other references to the wilderness throughout the Scripture). This wilderness, God's prepared place, is His place of security, which He promises to all true believers. God is not promising that Satan will not attack us by "striking our heel," as we studied. However, He has promised to nurture and protect our souls in those times. Part one of Revelation 12:11 proclaims that the victory has been won by the "blood of the Lamb," Jesus Christ. This was the deadly blow to Satan. However, part two states, "and the word of their testimony, and they loved their lives not unto the death." So it is clear that our fight against Satan requires us to claim and testify to the cleansing, redeeming, and overcoming power of the blood of Jesus Christ (our faith) and our willingness to sacrifice our earthly lives and passion to His purpose and cause.

In Revelation 12:14, we learn that Satan was sent back to earth to rule for a "short time." Even so, the Scripture states, the woman was given two wings of a great eagle so that she might fly quickly to the place prepared for her in the desert, where she would be taken care of and be out of Satan's reach. Again, we see God's promise to take care of His believers and keep them out of the enemy's reach. Many of us avoid exploring the many truths found in Revelation. This is terribly unfortunate, as it includes countless declarations made by God about

We cannot just wait and expect to conquer — be proactive knowing we have to knowing that's how it works!

Hope D. Blackwell

purpose, hope, victory, and protection for His true believers. I pray that you will walk in the power and victory already established for you and take full advantage of all God's promises for your life.

The book of Isaiah, being very prophetic, includes a scripture that I believe validates the book of Revelation. Isaiah 54:16, 17 declares:

> Behold, I have created the smith who blows the fire of coals, and produces a weapon for its purpose. I have also created the ravager to destroy; no weapon that is fashioned against you shall prosper, and you shall confute every tongue that rises against you in judgment. This is the heritage of the servants of the Lord and their vindication from me, says the Lord. (RSV)

Again, we see God's promises confirmed in His Word. He lets us know that He created the one who has forged a weapon to destroy us. God, the all-knowing and all powerful, has created the ravager but has denied him access to destroy us! He lets us know while the weapon may be fashioned against us, it will not succeed at causing our demise. When the very one who created the enemy is the one who guarantees your victory over him, rest assured, you have been called to conquer.

Purposeful Thoughts

★ Are we going to use this? Walk in it?

I declare that you are more than a conqueror, through the power of Jesus Christ. I destroy the strongholds of every situation that the enemy expected to result in defeat, depression, doom, confusion, and hopelessness in your life and the lives of those you influence. I use my God-given, Holy Ghost power via these written words to cause a change and shift in your soul, which speaks to the mind, will, and emotions. Through these written words, may God's Word of life be imparted to you at this very moment. He declares that you are not defeated. You are the head and not the tail. You are above and not beneath. You are healed, in Jesus's name!

I break the curse of the strongman produced by rejection, fear, and ignorance. According to the Word of God in Isaiah 61:3, I call forth the divine exchange of your garments; beauty for your ashes; the oil of joy for your mourning; and the garment of praise for your spirit of heaviness. I call you a tree of righteousness and pray for the manifestation of your every purpose and promise in the days ahead. I declare you blessed in the city, blessed in the field, blessed in your going out, and blessed in your coming in. I declare the fruit of your womb to be blessed in Jesus's name. You are called to conquer. Awake, arise, and clothe yourself with strength!

His Word to You

Woman of God, the enemy thought he had you bound and that in some way he had altered God's plan for your life. However, he himself has been deceived! Do not feel discouraged; you are in good company. He also had the same beliefs about the life of Jesus Christ. He thought the death of Christ was the end of everything because of his lack of omnipotence and foresight. At the time, he was unaware that the death of Christ had released the Holy Spirit, the third person of the trinity, and caused a multiplication through all who would accept and believe in Christ Jesus. Ha! You've got to love our strategic and omniscient God!

The same is occurring in your life right now. The enemy thought the divorce was your end, the depression was your end, the addiction was your end, the illness was your end, or perhaps even the form of godliness void of true power was your end. I declare to you, and to him, that it was only the beginning. Not only did it push you toward freedom and new life in Christ, it detonated the passion to snatch everyone else bound by your former demons and demand that Satan loosen his hold on them as well!

There are some God-given dreams, hopes, visions, and aspirations you thought had died and become only a memory of your past, but you must understand that you serve the God of resurrection. I declare that He has come to resurrect your dead dreams, hopes, and aspirations. I call you forth, out of the tomb of your mind, into your God-inspired purpose. I speak the words of life over you, that is, you will live and not die and declare the marvelous works of our Lord. We must remember that Jesus's most powerful miracles were demonstrated through the calling forth of dead situations and dead people. I say to you, as Jesus told Martha before He raised her brother from the dead, "if you will believe on this day, you shall see the glory of God"!

She became victorious by seeking him more - we cannot live stale lives if we desire change

Hope D. Blackwell

If there was ever a woman who was raised from the dead and can testify to the redemptive nature and power of God, I am she! Friend, I accepted Jesus Christ as my personal savior at age nine. I was gifted intellectually and spiritually, and people were always drawn to me and loved me, even when I was a child. Less than three months after I made the commitment to God and began to prepare myself spiritually, I was sexually abused. It was the summer; I was nine.

I engaged in abusive and promiscuous relationships beginning at age twelve, had three children by different young men by the time I was sixteen, and then got married, only to end up in a physically violent and emotionally abusive relationship. And that was only the beginning. I became a high-school dropout with three sons, was robbed and raped at gunpoint in a public place, attempted suicide on two occasions, divorced, had a fourth son out of wedlock who I put up for adoption. I was so tired and burdened by the time I was twenty-two, I could hardly endure, only to have my fifth child, a daughter.

But I felt the spirit of God drawing me into Him. I couldn't escape His love and His arms, which remained open. In my heart, I knew it was time for the deliverance and miracles I had often read and studied in the Word, even though there was the part of me that always felt my situation was too unique and too filthy to qualify for such blessings of God. Friend, I began to fast and pray, and slowly God began to change my desires, and I began to crave His Word and the fellowship I enjoyed with Him daily. God transformed me, but not without <u>extensive discipline</u> and due diligence on my part. As life continued, I grew in grace. While I faced times when I was overwhelmed and even disappointed, I knew God wanted me to open every door of my life and allow Him full access so he could perform a great work in me and my children. He wanted to raise me from the dead place! Friend, He removed the fear, shame, guilt, and stains of sin, once I received my full deliverance and embraced His love, mercy, and grace.

Indeed I faced challenges, and still do, even to this day. But nearly twenty years later, I have a transformed life filled with the love, peace, and grace of God, five great relationships with all of my wonderfully loving children, some of whom volunteer in our ministry. I have had the privilege of literally going all over the world, sharing God's never ending love for us through Christ Jesus, and His desire from the beginning to be our God and for us to be His people. I can say, "Now thanks be to

The Purposed Woman

God who always leads us to triumph in Christ, and through us diffuses the fragrance of His knowledge in every place. For we are to God the fragrance of Christ among those who are being saved and among those who are perishing" (2 Corinthians 2:13-15 (NKJV).

No matter how it looks, through Jesus Christ, you are more than a conqueror. The Word of God declares this:

> What, then, shall we say in response to these things? If God is for us, who can be against us? He who did not spare his own Son, but gave him up for us all—how will he not also, along with him, graciously give us all things? Who will bring any charge against those whom God has chosen? It is God who justifies. Who then is the one who condemns? No one. Christ Jesus who died—more than that, who was raised to life—is at the right hand of God and is also interceding for us. Who shall separate us from the love of Christ? Shall trouble or hardship or persecution or famine or nakedness or danger or sword? As it is written: for your sake we face death all day long; we are considered as sheep to be slaughtered; No, in all these things we are more than conquerors through him who loved us. For I am convinced that neither death nor life, neither angels nor demons, neither the present nor the future, nor any powers, neither height nor depth, nor anything else in all creation, will be able to separate us from the love of God that is in Christ Jesus our Lord. (Romans 8:31-39 NIV)

Daughter of God, all praise and glory be to God, for you and your every situation. I declare the Word of God in Romans 8:28 over your life, which tells us that all things shall work together for your good as you love God, and line up with His purpose for your life. That includes the good, the bad, and the ugly! My dear sister in Christ, you are truly more than a conqueror and a purposed woman. Guess what? No matter what life appears to be, when you are anchored in Jesus Christ and your purpose becomes whatever His purpose is for you, you win!

Devotional Notes

*Fight *be ready
*seize   *use your authority

Hope D. Blackwell

Purposeful Points from Chapter 5

1) Knowing that the enemy sets up strategies and traps for my demise, I will receive the victory that is mine through Christ Jesus. As with any war or "mutual opposition," I will break his authority by fighting with the spiritual weapons found in Ephesians 6:10-20!

2) In the Bible, from the book of Genesis through the book of Revelation, God has promised me victory in every battle I face. Even in my imperfections, God desires that I walk in the power and anointing of someone who is more than a conqueror in every situation. I will not be bound by my past or the lies of Satan. I will walk in purpose, beyond my limitations, seizing every opportunity I am given.

3) I must constantly be ready for battle, in a ready, aim, and fire mode. If I am not tuned in to Christ and led by the Spirit of God, I will take the hatred and opposition created within me, which was designed to be used against Satan, and fire it against people instead. I commit to focusing and obeying Proverbs 4:7, which states that "wisdom is the principal thing; therefore get wisdom, and with all thy getting, get understanding" (KJV).

4) There are some God-given dreams, hopes, and plans that seemed to be dead and just a memory of my past. But I understand that I serve the God of resurrection and life. I declare that He is resurrecting my once-dead hopes, dreams, and plans. Nothing is too hard for God. I declare and decree that it is done, and I am going forth in the pursuit of the purpose giver.

5) I will utilize the keys to the kingdom. These keys give me authority and access. God declares in Matthew 16:19: "And I will give unto you the keys to the kingdom of heaven; and whatsoever you shall bind on earth will be bound in heaven; and whatsoever you loose on earth will be loosed in heaven" (NKJV).

> Ye are of God, little children, and have overcome them: Because greater is He that is in you, than he that is in the world. (1 John 4:4 NKJV)

Chapter 6

The Spirit Woman

As women on the journey of purpose, we must recognize that in these times there is a need for the presence of what I call the "spirit woman." That simply signifies a woman who endeavors to consistently operate under the lead and direction of the Holy Spirit. This is not accomplished by womanly intuitions, outer beauty, or charm, but by submission to the Holy Spirit, who leads and guides into all truth. The spirit woman is a true Christian leader and example to all who interact with her. Without the presence of such a woman, there is an increased probability for misdirection, confusion, perversion, and utter chaos in the lives of those who need her guidance.

Despite the enemy's desires and attempts to destroy our lives and testimonies, we must become spirit women. While he would like our words to be empty and our lives to be powerless, that is not conceivable for spirit women, because our words and lives release life and truth. You may think this kind of lifestyle is unattainable, but I believe God went through great lengths to help us have these abilities, through Jesus's example and the Holy Spirit's residency within us. I am reminded of Proverbs 31:26: "The virtuous woman speaks with wisdom and faithful instruction is in her tongue" (NIV). As much as we can deceive ourselves into thinking that our actions do not affect the progress of others, the example we set has crucial ramifications, not only for our families but for generations to come, thus affecting the world. I am reminded of the spirit woman in my life, my dear mother, Virginia B. Blackwell, whose example of holiness and chaste conversation and manner not only marked each of her children's lives, but the lives of our children and their children. During foreign missions, I often think about how I am releasing the teachings that I received from my mother to countless lives across the world. Talk about living beyond the grave! As believers, we must understand that we are eternal creatures, and our lives on earth make a mark that travels far beyond what we think or imagine. As purposed women, it is imperative that we consider this in our daily living.

We must become purposed women who remain aware of the impact of our actions, be it positive or negative. Married women should be the support, balance, and protection for their husbands and family. As we studied in chapter 1, "Created for Purpose," you should be the giver of life, breathing life into your husband and family's visions, hopes, dreams, and aspirations. You should also create an atmosphere of peace and encouragement. Peter's instructions to wives include, "in like manner [of the man], be submissive to your husband's so that, if any of them do not believe the word, they may be won over without words by the behavior of their wives, when they see the purity and reverence of your lives" (1 Peter 3:1, 2 NIV). Under the leadership of the Holy Spirit, you have great power and influence. You can keep your husband before God through both your spirit-woman influence and prayer. It is then that you can release your concern about security, because you will develop the confidence that whatever he is instructed to do is of God.

For our children, we have a threefold ministry. We should be holy living examples, godly mothers, and loving wives. In early childhood, daughters aspire to be like their mothers so much that they memorize and imitate their gestures, comments, ideas, opinions, and beliefs. During my daughter's third and fourth-grade years in elementary school, she had a colorful children's Bible, a briefcase (as opposed to a regular backpack), and wanted a suit in every color that I had. She would walk across the street, and the crossing guard thought she was precious, walking around like a mini Hope D. Blackwell. The year after I wrote my first book, she published her first little book in elementary school. As women of purpose, we must recognize the seriousness of such observational learning. Although it was adorable, the Holy Spirit began to show me in greater magnitudes the power I was given to shape her life, and how He will hold me accountable for what I do with that power.

The years of early childhood development are the time when children are most impressionable. It is vital that we are conscious of this fact, with an awareness of what we say and do in front of our children. We must not allow our children to see us passively deal with the critical issues that go against our beliefs and values or indulge in the folly of this world and society at large. As purposed women of God, we cannot condone music, videos, literature, video games, internet sites, and media influences that glamorize sex, promiscuity, fornication, and adultery or glorify wealth, status, degrading and seductive styles of dress, obscene and vulgar language, and inappropriate dances and behavior. We must realize those things devalue our morals and Christian values, and rob our children of understanding their purpose in God. We must help them understand that God created various styles of music, but lyrics that are contrary to the Word of God will not be condoned or tolerated. Introduce them to positive alternatives to unhealthy rock and rap, and their related videos, and help them discover and create ways to have healthy childhoods while standing for righteousness and serving as examples. In order to do this, you must first sweep your own "house" clean.

We must also put our own media interest under scrutiny. Too often, they have sensual and sexually provocative tones as well as inappropriate jesting and language. Our passivity and indiscretions send the wrong messages to our children. It teaches them a diluted faith, void of the examples of truth, nullifying its true power and meaning in their lives. When we do this, we not only devalue our children, but we devalue the things of God, shaping our children into merely people of a religion, without the convictions that come from a relationship with God. Too often, we set our children up for failure by preaching one thing and doing another. By doing this, we actually train them to have only the form of godliness. When our children become overtaken by the things of the world, we are quick to ask, *How did this happen? Where did this come from? Why did you do this . . . after all I've taught you?* What are we really teaching? Are we simply raising a generation of religious people? We are the first representation of God that they see and experience. It is our responsibility to ensure they receive the right messages throughout their lives.

Adolescent daughters are being shaped to be future mothers. We must be sure that we are communicating love, affection, value, self-esteem, structure, accountability, and discipline. We have to be careful to maintain a balanced relationship with all of our children. We should value their thoughts, ideas, and opinions, but never allow them to usurp our authority. It is important that we chasten and correct them in order to create the structure and strength they will need for success as adults. We must look for opportunities to teach them practical spiritual principles through daily-life situations. When we function without the spirit of God, we leave them as prey for the world to feed on, making them lambs thrown among wolves.

Our sons need our protection, nurturing, and security. Daughters seek the security and protection of their fathers; however, our sons find this security in their mothers, while their fathers teach them the essentials of manhood. Generally, boys who feel deprived of their mother's security are likely to become more interested in girls earlier during adolescence. This is worsened when there is also no father present, and the effects can be devastating. When you add the sexual abuse that has become so common in families today, the devastation is multiplied. Homosexuality, promiscuity, rebellion, crime, and gang associations are just a few of the dangers that afflict children who lack parental support. We often talk about gangs without understanding of what attracts children to them. Unfortunately, Satan has taken basic family structure and perverted it in the form of gangs. If you look at the structure of a gang, underneath the chaos, it has some essentials that children seek within a family. There is an authority or strong leader. There is structure, accountability, what appears to be a family, and protection. There are also incentives or rewards for certain behaviors. There are rules and regulations, and ultimately what they perceive as love and sacrifice for "family members." When you examine it closely, it is sad. As adults, we blame the children without realizing the role that we play when we fail to structure our home with the same characteristics but in a Christian environment.

Woman of God, if our sons receive teaching, love, attention, belonging, structure, accountability, guidance, and discipline at home, they are more likely to be confident, make wiser decisions, choose healthy relationships, and select an appropriate mate with characteristics of their godly, purposed moms! They will also be more likely to honor women and treat them with love, understanding, and respect. Children will pick up our habits as well as our issues and, in most cases, exhibit some of the same behaviors. If we exhibit low self-esteem, our children may do so as well. If we are abusive or tolerate abuse, our children are more likely to do so. If we are sexually promiscuous, the same may be true of our children. As discussed in chapter 5, we must claim and walk in healing and wholeness to prohibit the impartation of brokenness to our posterity.

Unfortunately, today many parents are being replaced in their children's eyes by actors, musicians, sports icons, and other celebrities, who are exalted as modern-day idols. With the continued increase of single-parent homes, as well as the amount of time that many children spend outside the home, these deficient replacements continue to warp their minds through distorted depictions of success and prosperity. We can combat these lies and poor examples by taking the time to pray with our children and love, develop, and teach them in truth.

Women of God, it's time to be purposed in every way. We must play an active role in the restoration of the identity and purpose of our children. We must get back to Christ, where repentance, instruction, and healing can take place. It's time to embrace all the promises and plans of God for your life, and walk in your full potential as a godly spirit woman. You must be the suitable helper, life giver, and spirit woman who is diligent in building the kingdom of God for the return of Christ. It is time to develop a more intimate relationship with God, which is where you will find peace, wisdom, and power.

The enemy uses many lies to prevent women from developing an intimate relationship with God. God wants His women to be free from all self-created concepts and philosophies, many of which are the keys that have locked the doors upon women and kept them in bondage. For too long, women of God have been categorized and labeled according to the world's standards, based on size, shape, height, complexion, hair type and length, family status, education, occupation, and financial status. These, as well as many of the sayings listed below, are common diversions and misconceptions that have caused many women to walk in pain and error seeking the approval of others rather than the approval of God. The Bible instructs us in Matthew 6:33 to seek first God's kingdom and His righteousness, and all other things will be added to us. We must break away from the lies and statements that contradict the things that God says about us in His Word. Paul instructs believers in Romans 12:2 "And be not conformed to this world: but be ye transformed by the renewing of your mind, that ye may prove what is that good, and acceptable, and perfect, will of God" (KJV). As you replace these ideologies and falsehoods with the truth of God's Word, you will become empowered to walk in the newness of Christ.

Below are a few adages that have damaged women's self-worth, hearts, and minds. As you read these falsehoods, refute them with the Scriptures found in the Word of God.

Examples

False statement: It takes a woman to do a man's job.
Find the truth in Genesis 2:15, Galatians 3:28.

False statement: A woman's place is in the kitchen and the bedroom.
Find the truth in Proverbs 31:13-19, 24, 31.

False statement: It's okay to have sex as long as you love each other.
Find the truth in 1 Corinthians 6:18-20.

False statement: You have to use what you've got to get what you want.
Find the truth in Proverbs 31:30.

False statement: Women are beneath men.
Find the truth in Genesis 1:27.

False statement: You need a man for security.
Find the truth in Philippians 4:19.

False statement: A bird in the hand is worth two in the bush.
Find the truth in 2 Corinthians 5:7.

False statement: You're no good.
Find the truth in 1 Timothy 4:4.

False statement: You're not attractive enough.
Find the truth in 1 Peter 3:4, 5.

These are only a few of the lies that have been embedded in people's minds and perpetuated for generations. The falsehoods listed above, and many others, have misguided men and women in their walk with God, even after salvation. Remember, as mentioned in chapter 4, "In Pursuit of Purpose," the most important activity in the life of a spirit woman is prayer. Prayer is the key to all of our successes. When we pray, we invite God to change our situation for His glory. By way of prayer, we provide coverage for our husbands, children, families, brothers and sisters in Christ, sinners, the world, and the church. As the Word of God declares, the effective, fervent prayers of the righteous will avail. Woman of God, regardless of your current situation or circumstances, whether good or bad, God is calling you into a place in Him where you can know the truth, and the truth will make you free. The Word of God reminds us in Romans 8:28 "And we know that all things work together for good to them who love God, to them who are the called, according to His purpose" (KJV). God desires great things for you. He also desires that you take your assigned position in the mission of tearing down the kingdom of darkness and advancing the kingdom of God on earth for the return of Christ. God created you for a wonderful purpose that only you can fulfill. There are lives only you can touch! All of His intentions toward you are good and filled with promise. All you have to do is release the lies of the enemy, embrace the truth of God and His Word, and allow Him to bring you into alignment with

His purpose for your life. Again, remember the powerful declaration of God concerning your life found in Jeremiah 29:11-12:

> For I know the plans I have for you declares the Lord, plans to prosper you and not to harm you, plans to give you hope and a future. Then you will call upon me and come and pray to me, and I will listen to you. You will seek me and find me when you seek me with all your heart. I will be found by you, declares the Lord, and I bring you back to the place from which I carried you. (NIV)

Devotional Notes

Woman of God, you can succeed where Eve failed, because you have God's Word, Jesus's example, and the Holy Spirit's presence and power. You are called to be the head and not the tail, to be above and not beneath. God is so in love with you that in the midst of Eve's failure He made a way for your redemption. As discussed earlier in this book, the Word of God declares that through the seed of the woman (Jesus Christ), the authority of Satan was crushed and destroyed. And the benefits of the promise belong to you. You may have sinned, but just as God covered Adam and Eve, today He covers you through His only son, Jesus Christ, who became the sacrifice for the sins of all mankind. Jesus suffered, bled, and died for you and me. The great news is that He arose from the grave with all power in His hands and has given us access to God, eternal life, and power if we just believe on His name! He wants you to walk in the fullness of His love where peace, prosperity, and victory can overtake you. God needs you, other men and women need you, children need you, and this world needs you.

The Bible says in Luke 23:28-30:

> But Jesus, turning unto them said, "Daughters of Jerusalem, weep not for me but weep for yourselves, and for your children. For behold, the days are coming . . . which they

shall say, blessed are the barren, and the wombs that never bare, and the paps which never gave suck. Then they shall begin to say to the mountains, 'fall on us'; and to the hills, 'cover us.'" (KJV)

Jesus is referring to the devastating times that were to come and our need to lament and intercede for ourselves and those after us. Moreover, He is sharing that in subsequent generations, there will be great times of devastation and oppression, overwhelming and driving people to a place of depression and hopelessness. As we look around, we can clearly see these times approaching. I say to you, this is the time for the arising of the sons and daughters of God, those who are truly driven by His purpose. It is time for those end-time spirit women to sound the trumpet of truth and speak about the excellent things we discovered in Proverbs. The critical need for love, prayer, training, and teaching received from godly women cannot be stressed enough or neglected any longer. Look at, and hear the cries of, the increasing number of children in this generation who have not been given a godly foundation. As women of God, we must arise and stand in the gap and cry out in prayer, while preaching, teaching, comforting, and mothering.

God is looking for spirit women who will commune with Him, intercede for others, train future generations, and go when and where He instructs. The Bible declares in 2 Chronicles 16:9: "the eyes of the Lord run to and fro throughout the whole earth, to show Himself strong in the behalf of them whose heart is perfect toward him" (KJV). Release your heart before God, and be found by Him for such a time as this. Someone is waiting just for you. So, Woman of God, it's time to claim your healing, pursue your purpose, and arise as a purposed woman filled with God's spirit!

Friend, are you up for the challenge? Do you desire to be the one for whom God is searching to use for His great glory? The wonderful thing is you will never be alone. The purposed life is not always easy, but it is one of fulfillment, joy, and peace, and it is guaranteed for eternity! Let us agree in prayer:

> It is my prayer that a fresh wind of the Spirit will overtake you and usher you into a deeper place in Christ. I pray

that through these God-inspired words, you have been taught, challenged, encouraged, and provoked to further walk the Word of God and the will of God for your life. I pray that nothing will steal the words spoken into you during these times of reading, study, and devotion. I call forth the supernatural blessings of God to overtake you as you submit to His purpose. I pray that you will no longer walk under the curse of Eve, but in liberty through Jesus Christ, as a purposed woman. I call every crooked area of your life to be made straight as you walk in your future for the glory of God. I pray all darkness to be made light before you. I pray that you will meditate on the Word of God and that it will accomplish everything that it has been sent forth to do in your life, today and for eternity. In the name of Jesus, Amen.

Purposeful Points from Chapter 6

1) I will not operate according to the lusts of my flesh, but according to the Holy Spirit who dwells within me. I will be conscious of the power of my presence and influence in my home, community, marketplace, and ministry, and walk as an example of a virtuous woman, releasing life and love to all I encounter.
2) Embracing the calling of God as a woman of influence, I will use that influence to impart seeds of wisdom, life, hope, and promise in the lives of the next generation.
3) As a woman of God, I will be a channel through which God's blessings can flow, understanding that life is much bigger than my own personal successes, luxuries, and desires. I will accept the responsibility of being a spirit Woman, utilizing my time, gifts, and resources to share the love of Christ and improve the lives of others in various types of need.
4) I will be mindful of the purpose of God for my life as a woman and will release life in my dealings with others, no matter how dry or dead the situations appear. While I will weep with those who weep and rejoice with those who rejoice, I will release life and wisdom in all things.
5) I will honor God with my body, for it is the temple of the Holy Ghost. I will take care of myself, rest, eat properly, and flee all immoral acts.

> And now, my daughter, do not fear. I will do for you all that you request, for all the people of my town know that you are a virtuous woman. (Ruth 3:11 NKJV)

Chapter 7

Now Break Forth!

Woman of God, now that you know who you are, why you are, and more important, to whom you belong, there is only one thing left to do: BREAK FORTH! This chapter includes a prophetic Word from the book of Isaiah that presents instructions for obtaining the purpose of God for your life. It is filled with reassurance and encouragement as it reveals God's plan to remove the stains of guilt, shame, and reproach from His people, preparing them for a purposeful place of promise! His mercy is real, His grace is available, and His promises are true to those who obey His commands. As you read this Scripture, let it equip, encourage, and empower you to walk in a new place of victory and purpose as a purposed woman.

> Sing, O barren, thou that didst not bear; break forth into singing, and cry aloud, thou that didst not travail with child: for more are the children of the desolate than the children of the married wife, saith the Lord. Enlarge the place of thy tent, and let them stretch forth the curtains of thine habitations: spare not, lengthen thy cords, and strengthen thy stakes; For thou shalt break forth on the right hand and on the left; and thy seed shall inherit the Gentiles, and make the desolate cities to be inhabited. Fear not; for thou shalt not be ashamed: neither be thou confounded; for thou shalt not be put to shame: for thou shalt forget the shame of thy youth, and shalt not remember the reproach of thy widowhood any more. For thy Maker is thine husband; the

Lord of hosts is his name; and thy Redeemer the Holy One of Israel; The God of the whole earth shall he be called. (Isaiah 54:1-5 KJV)

1) Turn away from sin and unrighteousness and back to holiness

In order to be a channel in which the blessings of God can flow, you must first renounce unrighteousness and turn back to God. This promise of God in Isaiah is reserved for those who, after rebuke and judgment, will repent and turn back to God, who still loves us and is waiting to redeem, restore, and bless us.

- Although you are saved, in which areas of your life can you turn back to God? Where have you allowed other things to pull you away?

2) Worship, celebrate, and shout!

Sing, O barren, thou that did not bear. Break forth into singing and cry aloud thou that did not travail with child, for more are the children of the desolate than the children of the married wife, says the Lord. (Isaiah 54:1 KJV)

Barrenness is a state of unproductivity, unfruitfulness, and desolateness. According to Merriam Webster, barren means "habitually failing to fruit, or incapable of producing offspring." According to this verse, to go from barren to blessing, first you must sing! Singing speaks to worshipping, joyous expressions, and celebrating with praise. Don't allow the enemy to play a head game with you. Do not focus too much on the surrounding barrenness rather than on the greater one within you, who has not only the power to change you inside, but also the power to transform the barrenness around you. Your requirement is to sing, worship, and shout . . . in barrenness! A great songwriter said, "Don't wait until the battle is over, shout now!" The Scripture says the one who could never produce anything is the one who should break forth into a place of triumphant and victorious praise and worship, with confidence of the victory and blessings to come.

- How can worship help you in unproductive seasons? What awesome promise has God made to you in Isaiah 54:1?

3) Make preparations

> Enlarge the place of thy tent and let them stretch forth the curtains of thine habitations, spare not, lengthen thy cords, and strengthen thy stakes. (Isaiah 54:2 KJV)

<u>Enlarge your tent</u>

We often hear that there are three kinds of people:

- people who wish things would happen
- people who wonder what will happen
- people who make things happen

This is also true in the spiritual realm. "Enlarging your tent" speaks to making the necessary preparations to receive what God is doing. How long are you going to continue to hear God's Word, fail to personally receive it, or prepare and equip yourself to receive His blessings? Broaden your vision, and prepare your current dwelling for what God is going to do. We must ask ourselves whether we are in position and prepared to handle moving from worker to leader, from assistant manager to manager, from single to married, etc. Are you enlarging your vision, enlarging your habitations, and preparing for the blessing?

- What are practical ways to "enlarge your tent"?

Let them stretch forth the curtains of thine habitations!

Why does the verse say, "let them"? I used to wonder who were the "them" that Isaiah was referencing. They are your adversaries, those who are stretching, challenging, and opposing you. They are making you uncomfortable and forcing you to get in the presence of God, to get in position, and enlarge your capacity. They are the true "them" who are stretching the true you, the ones that you are praying about and asking God to get rid of!

Isaiah is telling us that instead of letting adversity or the adversary take you into a deeper barrenness, "let them stretch forth the curtains of thine habitations!" Let "them" no longer drive you from your blessing, but rather prepare you in such a way that allows God to pour even more into you. Talk about making your enemies your footstool! Sometimes you've got to be stretched and prepared before you can receive. I declare that some of your curtains are being stretched right now to position you for the blessings of God for your life.

- In which areas can you see God letting "them stretch forth the curtains" of the habitations in your life?

Lengthen your cords

Extend yourself! Do not remain where you are! I've learned through experience that the blessing can only go as far as you allow yourself to be extended or lengthened. We are often our greatest blessing blockers! God will not bless you with more than you are prepared to handle. There are no miracles in the comfort zone. Do you think it was comfortable for the woman with the issue of blood (mentioned in Mark 5:25) in her drained, weak condition to crawl through a crowd of people to get to Jesus? "Lengthening the cords" speaks to getting outside of your comfort zone. Faith will take you outside the zone; fear will keep you in it.

- What does "lengthening the cords" refer to in your life? How can you lengthen your cords?

Strengthen your stakes

Get strong, get matured, and get anchored! Strengthen the areas that used to break you easily. We are strengthened by declaring the Word and through intimacy, prayer, and study. You can't wait until you're in the middle of your adversity to get strong. That is too late! The Word of God declares that the joy of the Lord is your strength. If you have no strength, go back to step one and sing, worship, and sit at the feet of Jesus until your strength is renewed. Let me walk you through this: You have the tent, the cords, and the stakes. If the stakes are not strong, rooted, and anchored deep enough, they can be easily broken or uprooted. That is why this step is critical. If you enlarge the tent in preparation for more and lengthen the cords to accommodate the expectation, but fail to strengthen the stakes, friend, your work will be in vain. As soon as the storm comes, your stakes will get uprooted, and the tent will be destroyed, taking you back to square one! When this happens, we get angry with others and look for someone to blame for our catastrophes. However, in reality, often we aren't prepared and strong enough to handle what comes with increase. We must be prepared, matured, and anchored in the Word of God, which will keep us deeply rooted so that we aren't tossed to and fro with every strong wind that life that brings.

- How can you become stronger in preparation for the blessings of God for your life?

Watch God Move!

> For thou shall break forth on the right hand and on the left, and thy seed shall inherit the Gentiles and make the desolate cities inhabited. (Isaiah 54:3 KJV)

As God releases the promise, the Word of God declares that you will break forth on the right and the left and dispossess nations. In other words, you shall go into places where there are systems and people who aren't working in accordance with God's will. He will send you to dispossess, or take over, those places. This is what I call the "divine switcheroo." God is preparing you to take over some things for the advancement of His kingdom. He says further, "we will inhabit the desolate cities." In other words, He will send you to places that are dead and empty. But because you have positioned yourself according the Word of God, He is going to make things productive in once barren, desolate places. Don't despise the seemingly barren or desolate place. You are carrying resurrection power within you and a promise of God to bring forth something out of nothing. Because of preparation, God will cause you to prosper in the place that was unproductive, uninhabited, and downright messed up! God is saying, "I am sending you to some places that look desolate. But don't be deceived; it's me, and it's blessed." Believe!

- What can you do to populate the "desolate cities" in your life and the lives of others?

Fear Not!

> Fear not; for thou shall not be ashamed, neither be thou confounded, for thou shall not be put to shame; thou shall forget the shame of thy youth and remember the reproach of thy widowhood no more. (Isaiah 54:4 KJV)

Too often, our pasts have been so difficult, or our lives so barren or unfruitful, they have sparked fear and unbelief in our hearts. The spirit of fear and remembrance of our past unproductive lives and sins make us ashamed, confounded, and condemned, feeling as if transformation is impossible. This causes us to develop an unconscious readiness to give up on the blessings and the promise of God. The Bible declares, "there is now therefore no condemnation to them which are in Christ Jesus who walk not after the flesh but after the spirit" (Romans 8:1 NKJV), and "I am he that blotteth out your transgressions and for mine own sake I will not remember thy sins" (Isaiah 3:25 KJV). He can't ruin what He's doing for His own glory, so there is a removal of sin that is done at the time of repentance. My friend, you must not fear! The enemy is trying to trick you into self-condemnation and make you feel as though you will fail or be embarrassed. He wants you to feel that your past is so horrendous, you will never walk in a future filled with promise. The Bible says if we confess our sins, He will be faithful and just and will forgive us and cleanse us from all unrighteousness. Fear not!

- Too often we fear great things because we still are bound by the past or won't believe enough to walk in God's promise. What lies must you leave behind?

God Is Your Provider

> Thy maker is thine husband, the Lord of Host is his name; and thy Redeemer is the Holy One of Israel, the God of the whole earth shall he be called. (Isaiah 54:5 KJV)

The very one who created you, redeemed you, and restored you is now married to you. Your provider, Jehovah Jireh, God Almighty, the Savior of the world, is joined to you in promise and covenant. He is not a man that He should lie. God reminds us that regardless of past barrenness, we have a Redeemer! We must remember with whom we are in covenant, and then walk in confidence, knowing that we aren't doing it, He is!

- God is the faithful husband. How will you find comfort from His promises in this Scripture?

Purposeful Points from Chapter 7

1) I will rid my life of sin and idolatrous behaviors, turn toward God, and live a lifestyle of holiness that is pleasing to Him and representative of His presence in my life.
2) In seemingly low and unproductive seasons, I will purpose myself to continue in the attitude of worship and gratitude to God. I will press through times of unfruitfulness and break forth into singing and joyous celebration. Proverbs 31:25 says "Strength and honor are her clothing, and she shall rejoice in the time to come" (KJV).
3) I will prepare myself to receive all that God intends in my life by enlarging my current boundaries, stretching myself outside of my current comfort zone, and strengthening myself by developing, enduring, and maturing in my walk with God and in my life situations.
4) I will allow God to be God in situations and circumstances rather than worry about and get involved in matters that are higher than I am. I will have confidence in my maker!
5) I will renounce fear in the understanding that God didn't give me a spirit of fear, but of power, love, and a sound mind. I will recognize that fear is a spirit and not a feeling, and break the grip of it through the power of prayer.
6) I will be cognizant of the covenant relationship I have with the God of the whole earth, who is my provider and more than able to save, deliver, heal, and restore me.

> Now to Him who is able to do exceedingly abundantly above all that we ask or think, according to the power that works in us, to Him be glory in the church by Christ Jesus to all generations, forever and ever. Amen. (Ephesians 3:20 NKJV)

Conclusion

The Only Way to a Purposed Life

Perhaps you have read this book and realize that you have never accepted Jesus Christ into your heart as your personal Lord and Savior. Maybe you grew up in church or experienced religious traditions void of an authentic and personal relationship with God through Jesus Christ. Maybe you walked away from God because of some disappointment, violation, or deep pain caused by a misunderstanding. Perhaps you just never embraced the truth of the Bible, which is the written Word of God. Quite possibly, you were never extended an invitation to accept Jesus Christ, the son of God, into your heart. Too often we spend time condemning and judging rather than sharing the message of the unconditional love of God and His great mercy and grace toward us all.

Friend, no matter how great or disappointing life may seem, know that the only way to a truly purposed life is to return to the one who gave you a purpose before you were even born! Friend, did you know you were created and uniquely designed by God for a great and wonderful purpose that is found only through relationship with Him? It is God's will to be in a loving relationship with you and bring you into His great plans.

> For I know the thought that I think toward you, says the Lord, thoughts of peace and not evil, to give you hope and a future. (Jeremiah 29:11 NIV)

It is true, my friend, God has these plans for you. God is the creator of all life, and every life was created for a purpose. In the beginning, when God created everything, He said it was good. So guess what? God started something really good when He formed you. Regardless of where life has taken you, it is His desire to complete that good work in and through you.

> Being confident of this very thing, that He which has begun a good work in you will perform it until the day of Jesus Christ . . . (Philippians 1:6 KJV)

No matter who you are or what you've done, God loves you and desires to be in relationship with you. His love and desire for you is so great that He sent His only son, Jesus Christ, to die for your sins to redeem you back to Him. This means everything that separates you from Him has been removed because of Jesus Christ. You can have access to God, and walk in fellowship with Him, as He intended from the beginning of time. Jesus took responsibility for all of your sins and wrongdoings; through His death, burial, and resurrection, you now have a right to this new, abundant, and eternal life in God.

> For God so loved the world that He gave His only begotten Son, that whoever believes in Him should not perish but have everlasting life. For God did not send His Son into the world to condemn the world, but that the world through Him might be saved. (John 3:16, 17 NKJV)

It is simple. God doesn't force anything on us. Although He lets us know clearly in John 14:6 that no man comes to the Father except through Jesus Christ, he still gives us free will to choose. By faith do you believe these glorious truths in your heart? Are you ready to walk in new and eternal life in Jesus Christ? If so, pray this prayer out loud: Jesus, I'm a sinner and I want to be saved. I believe you are the son of God, you died on the cross for my sins, and you were raised from the dead with all power. Come into my heart, save me, and fill me with your Spirit. At this moment, I give you my life for the rest of my life. In the name of Jesus, Amen.

> . . . that if you will confess with your mouth the Lord Jesus, and believe in your heart that God has raised him from the dead, you will be saved. For with the heart man believes unto righteousness, and with the mouth confession is made unto salvation. (Romans 10:9-10 NKJV)

There is nothing that we can ever do to earn our salvation. It is by His grace, a gift from God. Although it costs us nothing, it cost Him everything. As undeserving as we are, His great love and purpose release this unmerited grace to us in that if we believe in the son of God, we too are made children of God.

> For by grace you have been saved through faith, and that not of yourselves; it is the gift of God, not of works, lest anyone should boast. For we are His workmanship, created in Christ Jesus for good works, which God prepared beforehand that we should walk in them. (Ephesians 2:8-10 NKJV)

Jesus has forgiven you and has set you free from the bondage of sin. You are saved and free. No longer allow the enemy to hold you hostage because of your past. Your past has passed, and now God is moving you into an eternal and glorious future that has many promises. Walk in the liberty and new life that you have received through Christ Jesus.

> "I, even I, am he who blots out your transgressions, for my own sake, and remembers your sins no more" (NIV). (Isaiah 43:25)

Wow, friend, now your life has no end! While you will leave the earth, you will experience new life in eternity where you will fellowship with God daily. The remainder of your life is simply preparation for the quality of your eternity in heaven, where you will be rewarded for the work you do on earth in the name of the Father.

> Yes, we are fully confident, and we would rather be away from these earthly bodies, for then we will be at home with the Lord. So whether we are here in this body or away from this body, our goal is to please him. For we must all stand

before Christ to be judged. We will each receive whatever we deserve for the good or evil we have done in this earthly body. (2 Corinthians 5:8-10 NLT)

Friend, welcome to the family! I've been praying for you and awaiting your arrival. You were created to fulfill a purpose in this kingdom, and as you walk with God, He will reveal it to you. Give Him genuine lordship over your mind, body, soul, and life, and you'll never be the same again! More important, through the gift of eternal life through Jesus, God has done more for you than you could ever imagine because He has changed your eternal dwelling place from the eternal damnation of hell to the everlasting joy of heaven

Afterword

Beloved Sister in Christ,

It is my deepest hope and prayer that your life has been changed forevermore through these God-inspired words for your life. I pray that this book inspired you to walk in a lifelong journey filled with intentionality, meaning, and purpose. It is my prayer that you be equipped, encouraged, and empowered to walk victoriously in God's purpose for your life as a suitable helper and woman of worth in the kingdom of God. You are a purposed woman, and it is time for you to arise in the victory that has been given to you through the life, death, and resurrection of Jesus Christ. Allow God to be the driver during the journey, and learn to enjoy the ride. Remember, with Christ, you're always going somewhere filled with purpose. His Word declares that He has good plans for you, which will give you a hope and a future.

I say to you as Paul said to the Ephesians in Ephesians 1:15-19:

> Therefore I also, after I heard of your faith in the Lord Jesus and your love for all the saints, do not cease to give thanks for you, making mention of you in my prayers: that the God of our Lord Jesus Christ, the Father of glory, may give to you the spirit of wisdom and revelation in the knowledge of Him, the eyes of your understanding being enlightened; that you may know what is the hope of His calling, what are the riches of the glory of His inheritance in the saints, and what is the exceeding greatness of His power toward us who believe, according to the working of His mighty power (NKJV).

I pray further that you will fully embrace the many rich blessings of the Lord, which add no sorrow. I declare that you will not be conformed to this world, but will be transformed by the renewal of your mind. You shall become the proof of the good, perfect, and acceptable will of God on the earth. I pray you will walk in the manifest presence, peace, power, and purpose of Almighty God all the days of your life.

I would love it if you would e-mail me at salvation@hopeblackwell.com so I can send you a special Word of encouragement in your new purposeful journey. I look forward to hearing from you soon!

Hope D. Blackwell

Made in the USA
Lexington, KY
24 May 2014